Success with

Climbers & Creepers

CLAUDIA KRINNER

Series Editor:
LESLEY YOUNG

Contents

Nasturtiums are ideal for covering a fence with greenery and flowers.

Kiwi fruit flowers.

Morning glory requires plenty of sun.

Cover photographs
Front cover: *Clematis.*
Back cover: *Virginia creeper (top), honeysuckle (bottom left), flowering ivy (bottom right).*

3

Foreword

Houses and other buildings may be made of concrete and brick but all around them carefully cultivated flower beds, patios, and balconies and lovingly tended rockeries and hedges bear witness to a human longing to be close to nature. Nowadays many gardens are quite small and patios and balconies do not often provide enough space for all the pots, containers, and boxes one might wish. The best way to overcome this lack of lateral space is to make good use of the vertical by letting plants grow and flower on a façade and, at the same time, cover boring buildings, concrete walls, and plain fences with greenery. If permitted, in time plants will creep and climb up several storeys, filling the space between a balcony and a roof, above an entrance door and around windows.

This colorful guide will tell you how to make the outside of your house more attractive by using climbing plants. Here you will find numerous ideas for greenery to cover any structure.

Author Claudia Krinner, an expert on climbers and garden design, explains which plants are particularly suited to covering a house or balcony with greenery. She supplies detailed, individual instructions on plant care and reveals which plants will flourish both in the garden and also in large containers. Popular climbing plants, like clematis, ivy, Virginia creeper, grapevine, cathedral bell, climbing roses and many others, are shown to full advantage in the lovely color photographs.

Most plants need some form of climbing aid and in order to help the reader to choose and construct the best one for each plant, this volume supplies precise instructions and step-by-step illustrations on the use and securing of the right support. Enchanting flowers in the spring and juicy apples, pears, apricots or peaches in the fall offer a splendid return for the effort of establishing espaliers. All you need to know about planting and caring for fruits grown in this way against a house wall can be found in a separate, detailed chapter.

To ensure success in the planting of new climbers, the author has provided useful advice on choosing the right position, the best compost and growing mediums, the right way to plant, both in open soil and in large containers, and on watering and fertilizing. Notes are also given on the use of biological plant protection agents, while step-by-step, full-color illustrations help to convey practical gardening knowledge.

One point that often concerns the amateur gardener is the danger of damage to a house wall or other structure when climbers are grown and the author has covered this topic fully, so that you can feel free to go ahead and cover an entire wall with climbing roses, ivy or a grapevine. Finally, do not forget that "green" walls not only create beauty and a special atmosphere around a house, they also provide shelter and food for many fascinating creatures.

The author
Claudia Krinner has a diploma in landscape gardening and is an expert on garden design and the use of climbing plants.

Author's notes
This volume deals with the planting and care of climbing plants and creepers on the outside walls of buildings. Some of the plants described here are toxic and the instructions for individual care on pages 39-59 indicate this by means of a special symbol. Please make absolutely sure that children and domestic pets are not able to eat toxic plants as they may seriously damage their health.

Also make certain that all climbing aids and espaliers are well secured to avoid the risk of accidents or injury.

A house smothered in luxuriant greenery
Many climbing plants, like the Virginia creeper shown here, manage to cover entire walls in a relatively short time.

Plants and climbing aids

There is no finer sight than a house wall covered by the leaves of a fiery-colored creeper or enveloped in a mass of green foliage, unless it is a balcony adorned with a colorful, scented cloud of flowers or a patio that is reminiscent of the warm Mediterranean. It may be every gardener's dream but it is an ambition that is easier to turn into reality than you might believe. The range of suitable climbing plants is huge and the right climbing aids are easy to install.

Planting climbing plants around the outside of your home will give it a completely new appearance. The widespread use of climbers can also play a part in improving the general atmosphere of a town and will provide both a habitat and food for many small creatures. Without the need for a great deal of equipment or even special knowledge, you can disguise an ugly corner or adorn the shady side of a building with flowering climbing plants, evergreen ivy, or Virginia creeper, covering every surface, from house façades, balconies and patios to above entrance doors and around windows, right through to gutters and composting sites.

Plants for housewalls

The success of your "green" house exterior will largely depend on your selection of the right plants.
Climbing plants: With only a little effort, and in a very short time, some climbers will completely cover ugly façades or large expanses of unsightly wall. Such plants are also suitable for providing greenery on a balcony, on fences, and in the garden. One important point to note is that plants have different ways of climbing and will, therefore, require different types of climbing support. Relatively few climbing plants can manage without this.
Fruit espaliers have long been a popular way of growing fruit trees against a wall or fence.
Bushes and hedges: Planted along a fence or the side of a patio, bushes and hedges are excellent for providing shelter or a visual screen. Many species make a home for birds, small mammals, and insects, and thereby contribute to the protection of nature and encourage wildlife in the garden.
Large container plants are an ideal way of providing greenery in positions where you cannot plant directly into the ground.
Many climbing plants are also suitable for planting in large containers or pots.
Summer flowers can be planted in balcony boxes to create greenery and color anywhere. These are usually annuals which can be sown as seed or planted as young plants obtained from garden centers or nurseries.

Buying plants

Growing in the right position is particularly important for the healthy development and growth of plants. The mini-climate will vary in different spots so that different conditions will be experienced by plants growing outside, in garden flower beds or against a house wall than by plants grown in a large container or balcony box (see p. 21).

Climbing plants which flourish in large containers
black-eyed Susan (*Thunbergia alata*)
cathedral bell (*Cobaea scandens*)
clematis (*Clematis*)*
convolvulus (*Convolvulus sepium*)*
cucumber (*Cucumis sativus*)
hop (*Humulus lupulus*)
ivy (*Hedera helix*)*
kiwi fruit (*Actinidia chinensis*)
morning glory (*Ipomoea tricolor*)*
nasturtium (*Tropaeolum*)
ornamental gourd (*Cucurbita pepo var. ovifera*)
rose (*Rosa*)
Russian vine (*Fallopia baldschanica*)
scarlet runner bean (*Phaseolus coccineus*)*
spindleberry (*Euonymus fortunei*)*
sweet pea (*Lathyrus odoratus*)*
Virginia creeper (*Parthenocissus quinquefolia* and *P. tricuspidata*)
(*toxic plants)

6

isteria will flourish in a sheltered position on the south- or west-facing side of the house.

The most important points to consider when choosing plants are light, temperature, soil, and water.

You will find detailed information on the individual requirements of many climbing plants on pages 9-59.

Perennial climbing plants or woody plants do not die back in the winter. Instead, they form woody shoots. These plants are usually sold as young plants in containers or pre-grown in pots. Shrubs can also be obtained as

rooted plants and are usually cheaper when bought this way as they do not have a firm rootstock. They may take rather longer to become established than plants bought with a proper rootstock.

My tip: Before planting, make sure that you undo the twine securing the cloth around the rootstock so that it cannot strangle the neck of the root.
Annual climbing plants or summer flowers can be pre-grown in pots or bought as seed.

They will not survive the winter and will have to be re-sown or bought as young plants again the following spring.
Summer-green, deciduous woody plants (like Virginia creeper), whether bought as a small plant in a pot or with a rootstock and protective covering, are best acquired when they have no leaves. This will help the plant to establish itself more easily as it does not lose so much water through evaporation when it is leafless.

Unfortunately, you will not be able to tell at this stage whether you have purchased a healthy, robust plant. Plants like hops or bindweed, which have a rootstock and have been pre-grown in a pot, are also obtainable from garden centers. The parts of the plant that are above ground will die off in the winter; the underground parts will form new shoots in spring.

When purchasing **plants for espaliers**, it is important to consider the height of the trunk of the plant. This is the distance between the neck of the root to the beginning of the crown which is where the plant begins to branch out.

Remember where the windows are in a house wall when working out where to plant an espalier.

Climbing techniques
Hops (left) and other winding plants require vertical supports; plants which have adapted their leaf stalks for climbing, like the clematis (right), grow best on grid-like frames.

Climbing techniques
Virginia creeper (Parthenocissus quinquefolia, left) is a plant with suckers. The climbing rose (right) is a rambler which holds on with its thorns.

How to recognize healthy plants
● By their leaves. In the case of large container plants and summer flowers, a good healthy green color will generally indicate that the plant is not suffering from any deficiencies.
● By the bark which should be completely undamaged. Cuts in the stem that are the result of work done to improve the shape of the plant do not fall into this category. However, any such marks should look clean and some protective tissue should already have grown over them.
Pests and diseases (see p. 34) should never occur on quality stock.
When purchasing woody plants, remember to check for rust. This is recognizable by tiny, bright red bumps on the bark. Even healthy plants can be infected.

Where to purchase plants
The best place to go is a reputable plant or tree nursery run by professional gardeners. Here, in addition to quality stock, you will also be able to obtain expert advice. You will find the addresses of local nurseries in your telephone directory. You can also purchase a directory of nurseries and plant specialists in most good bookshops, or write to the inquiries page of a reputable gardening magazine (enclose a stamped, self-addressed envelope).
Garden centers: In addition to offering a similar selection to tree nurseries, good garden centers should also have a large selection of accessories for sale.
Mail order companies also offer a wide selection of plants. Whenever you order something from a catalog, do make sure that it will come from a reputable source so that you will be certain to receive genuinely fresh stock.
Markets and other venues often offer interesting opportunities to stock your own garden or balcony with new plants, but do check such plants carefully for signs of disease or pests.

How plants climb
Whatever support plants find in nature to help them to climb from the shady ground up to the light, is what you will have to provide artificially around your house or on your balcony.
NB: The type of climbing aid should be chosen to suit the individual climbing technique of the plant. There are plants that wind, plants with tendrils, plants with root suckers and those that ramble.
NB: Various kinds of climbing aid can be obtained to suit these respective climbing techniques (see p. 11). These climbing frames or grids must be fixed to the wall before planting. The minimum space between the house wall and the climbing aid should be at least 4 in (10 cm).

Plants that wind
Most climbing plants belong to the group of winding plants which climb up the support by using the whole shoot. These plants always wind around their support in one direction only, so a distinction must be made (when viewed from above) between:
● left-winding plants which grow anti-clockwise and are most common, and

● right-winding plants (only a few) which grow clockwise, such as hops and honeysuckle.

Climbing aids for winders:
Plants that wind require vertical supports such as sticks, strings, or wires.

It is important to choose a support with the correct diameter. Support sticks with a diameter of 1¼-2 in (3-5 cm) are suitable for most winders. A support with a much larger diameter, from about 4 in (10 cm) upward, would be too big for the winding shoot of *Wisteria* to encircle, for example. If the climbing aids are too thin, on the other hand, very vigorous winders, like Russian vine, may strangle themselves.

Vertical crosspieces between the individual support sticks are merely intended to strengthen the frame and to prevent the plants from sliding down the smooth surface of the support. If you wish a shoot to grow sideways, it will have to be trained and tied (see, p. 29).

Annual winders
black-eyed Susan (*Thunbergia alata*)
morning glory (*Ipomoea tricolor*)*
scarlet runner bean (*Phaseolus coccineus*)*

Perennial winders
Akebia quinata
Celastrus orbiculatus*
Dutchman's pipe (*Aristolochia macrophylla*)
honeysuckle (*Lonicera*)*
hop (*Humulus lupulus*)
kiwi fruit (*Actinidia chinensis*)
Russian vine (*Fallopia baldschuanica*)
wisteria (*Wisteria sinensis*)*

(*toxic plants)

Plants with adhesive pads and root suckers
Virginia creeper (*Parthenocissus tricuspidata* "Veitchii," left) climbs with the help of adhesive pads; ivy (right) uses root suckers.

My tip: Winders require enough space to encircle their support. Wall spacers (see illustration, p.13) will ensure the necessary gap between the wall and the frame (minimum distance 12 in/30 cm).

Plants with tendrils
These plants climb by using specially adapted organs, for example, either with the help of specially adapted long leaf stalks, like the clematis (*Clematis*), or by using tendrils which evolved through an adaptation of the shoots, as in the case of the grapevine (*Vitis vinifera*).
There are:
● plants which climb by means of long leaf stalks that are sensitive to pressure
● plants with suckers, which use their slender shoots purely for climbing
● plants with tendrils, which have developed additional adhesive pads on the tips of their shoots to help them to climb without any other kind of aid. These include some forms of Virginia creeper (*Parthenocissus tricuspidata* "Veitchii" and *Parthenocissus quinquefolia* "Engelmannii") which only grow a few adhesive pads.

When stimulated by pressure or touch, these pads secrete minute quantities of an adhesive which hardens on exposure to air.

Climbing aids for plants with tendrils: Net or grid-shaped climbing aids made of wood, wire, twines, or builders' reinforcing mesh. Grids, wire mesh, and wires may be arranged vertically, horizontally or even diagonally.
● The individual sticks of a grid or frame should not be too thick as the tender shoots would find it too difficult to wind around them.

Annuals with tendrils
cathedral bell (*Cobaea scandens*)
nasturtium (*Tropaeolum majus, T. peregrinum*)
ornamental gourd (*Cucurbita pepo var. ovifera*)
sweet pea (*Lathyrus odoratus*)*

Perennials with tendrils
clematis (*Clematis*)*
grapevine (*Vitis vinifera*)
Virginia creeper (*Parthenocissus quinquefolia, P. tricuspidata*) (*toxic plant)

● In the case of delicate plants, for example those that use extended leaf stalks, like nasturtium, the mesh gauge of a grid should not be more than 2 by 2 in (5 by 5 cm).

Plants with root suckers
Plants may also climb with the help of their roots, for example ivy. As soon as it comes into contact with a firm base, ivy produces special adhesive roots straight out of the shoots just beneath a leaf stalk.
Being "true climbing plants," plants with root suckers do not require any kind of climbing aid.

Plants with root suckers
ivy (*Hedera helix*)*
hydrangea (*Hydrangea petiolaris*)
spindleberry (*Euonymus fortunei*)*
trumpet vine (*Campsis radicans*)
(*toxic plants)

y tip: Young plantlets like to use
short piece of twine or a stick
ning diagonally against the wall
a means of getting started in the
ht direction.

mblers
mblers like the climbing rose
osa) are not equipped with
ecially adapted climbing
gans. Instead, they produce
g, flexible shoots, usually also
uipped with thorns or prickles,
help them to climb up the
ger supporting plants that they
d onto. If they cannot find
ough support themselves or
ir own weight pulls them down,
wever, it will be necessary to
pply them with additional
mbing aids.

neysuckle covering an arch
s vigorous climber soon covers
arched climbing frame with a
fusion of summer flowers.

Climbing aids for ramblers: Use
grids or frames with as many
vertical battens as possible, for
example, diagonal grids. These
plants cannot climb by
themselves so their new shoots
have to be woven into the frame
or tied up from time to time.

Ramblers
blackberry (*Rubus*)
rose (*Rosa*)
winter jasmine (*Jasminum nudiflorum*)

Materials

As a rule, erecting climbing aids is
not something for which you will
need planning permission but it is
always a good idea to ask your
landlord if you are renting a home.
The case is different if the building
is an historic one and this point
should be checked with the
relevant authority.

Support sticks
Support sticks made of wood,
plastic, metal, or plastic-coated
metal are among the simplest
types of climbing aid. They can be
arranged in a pattern or woven
together with the help of wire or
twine, or you can stand several
sticks in such a way that they
meet at the top.
Use: These are ideal for winding
plants, like scarlet runner beans,
black-eyed Susan or Russian vine.
Securing: Lightweight sticks for
supporting annual winders should
be driven about 20 in (50 cm) deep
into the soil. More stable sticks can
be set in holes 20-32 in (50-80 cm)
deep, perhaps even cementing
them in if they are intended to

---

support very vigorously growing
climbing plants like Russian vine.
Drive the sticks into the compost in
a pot or large container if the
plants are to grow in pots.

Ropes or twine made from natural fibers
Ropes made of hemp, sisal or
coconut fiber can be obtained
from gardening suppliers. They
are plant-friendly and provide a
firm grip as they have a rough
surface. Their durability will be
somewhat limited, however, if
they are used outdoors. They tend
to expand in increased humidity
so the support they give to the
plants can become too loose.
Use: For annual winders.
Securing: Knot them to screw-in
eyes or to rings that can be
dowelled into the house wall.

Plastic rope
It is essential to use twine or rope
with a rough surface as a climbing
aid in order to prevent the plant
from sliding down. Nylon hop
ropes, ¾-in (15-mm) thick, can be
obtained in the trade. These ropes
have a rough surface, are cheap,
can be straightened out quite
easily with a simple stretcher
(obtainable from hardware stores),
and will last a long time.
NB: Vigorously growing winders
may become too heavy for these
ropes.
Use: For perennial winders like
kiwi fruit and hops.
Securing: Fasten them to the
house wall in the same way as
rope made of nylon (see above).

Wire rope
Because of their strength, wire
ropes can be used to bridge
larger gaps. Galvanized or plastic-
coated stainless steel wire will
have sufficient anti-rusting
qualities.

To prevent winders from sliding down smooth surfaces of vertical supports, provide horizontal supports, install screw-on wire rope clamps at regular intervals to act like "knots," or rough up the plastic coating.
Use: For winders like hops and Dutchman's pipe.
Securing: These must be fixed securely because of the load on the support. A tripod dowelled into the wall at the top end of the rope/wire should be sufficient. Anchoring the rope/wire in the soil can be achieved with the help of a point anchor made of concrete or heavy, galvanized metal plates. Use metal eyelets that have been cast in, welded on or screwed on (see illustration above).
Use various kinds of stretchers to pull the rope taut (obtainable from builders' merchants or from hardware stores; remember to indicate the gauge of wire you are using):
● simple wire stretchers for ropes less than 10 ft (3 m) long; these can only be tightened by a maximum of 10 in (25 cm).
● locking stretchers for use with thicker wire and rope to a length of over 10 ft (3 m). Thinner rope ends should be tidily twisted together using pliers at the junction point with the stretcher. Thicker wire ropes are best taken to a professional ropemaker where the ends are placed in soft metal capsules and then sealed together under great pressure.

Plastic-coated grids
Garden centers can supply a good stock of plastic grids and plastic-coated metal wire, including tools, as ready-to-buy items. They are easy to assemble and are normally treated against rusting by the manufacturers.
Uses: For plants with tendrils and

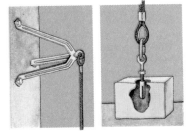

Fixing wire supports
At the top end, a tripod has been dowelled into the wall (left). A point anchor made of concrete is used to anchor the wire into the ground.

winders like *Clematis* or smaller climbing roses. These grids would rapidly end up being too small for vigorously growing plants like *Wisteria* or Russian vine.
Securing: Hang on wall spacers with dowelled wall hooks (see illustration, p. 13)

Builders' reinforcing mesh and wire-mesh grids
Builders' reinforcing mesh can be bought in sections of 8 by 17 ft (2.5 by 5 m) in builders' merchants. Use a strong metal saw or a bolt cutter for cutting the mesh to size. This mesh is easy to shape into arches or pergolas or to fix to walls as a flat climbing aid. Note that it will need a coat of anti-rust paint.
Wire-mesh frames are also suitable as climbing aids. The wire mesh is very cheap and is usually galvanized. It will be even stronger if it is set into a strong wooden frame and fixed with U-shaped steel nails (see illustration, p. 13).
Use: For winders like *Clematis*, sweet peas or nasturtiums.
Securing: Install in the same way as plastic grids (see above).

Wood
Wooden frames or grids are still the most popular element for supporting green climbing plants because of their natural look, plant-friendly qualities, and the multitude of possibilities for use.
Use: For perennial winding plants and plants with tendrils.

My tip: The diameter of wooden battens may sometimes be too large and additional horizontal twines or thinner wooden battens will have to be provided as climbing aids.

NB: Climbing frames made of wood should not be in direct contact with the soil which might cause the wooden parts to start to decay from the bottom up (it is a good idea to secure them in concrete with a "metal shoe").
Wood protection agents: Treating the wood with a protection agent before installation is recommended. Try to use biological wood protection agents as they are less harmful to humans and plants. They include: linseed oil, wood oil, wood tar, soda, and natural resins. You can also obtain pigments (in powder form) for mixing with the agent to obtain a colorful finish.
Pressure-treated woods (the protection agent is driven into the wood under high pressure) are good for use as posts or weight-bearing supports with a larger diameter. They should not, however, contain substances that are harmful to plants, such as phenols, chlorine, or ammonium hydroxide. When purchasing wood, ask which agents have been used to treat it.
The most important points to remember when using wood are:
● Use high-quality wood with few knotholes.
● Cover up exposed ends with plastic or metal strips to protect them against rain.

The use of planed wood will
increase the risk of the wood
becoming soaked right through.
The unprotected ends of posts
should be cut off at an angle so
that water can run off more easily.
Grids made of wood: These can
easily be made out of roof battens
which can be obtained from a
timber yard or builder's merchant
in a range of diameters from ¾ by
1½ in (2 by 4 cm) to 1½ by 2½ in
(4 by 6 cm) and in lengths of 7-20
ft (2-6 m), either rough-cut or
planed, in a natural, untreated
state or pressure-treated. Even
without any experience of
woodwork, you will find them easy
to assemble into the desired grid
pattern and they are very cheap
to buy. When constructing a
wooden grid, nail, screw, or glue
the battens together both
horizontally and vertically. Use
rustfree wire pegs or a
weatherproof glue or screws.
Securing: Use dowels for fixing
hooks into the wall. Use metal or
plastic capsules as spacers.
Pieces of cork will do equally well
if the spaces are small.

Climbing frames made of metal

Metal structures, made from steel
tube, for example, and properly
treated against rusting, are very
durable and strong. They are
especially useful for creating free-
standing, three-dimensional or
curved climbing frames.
It will be necessary to tie the
plants on. Such elaborate
climbing frames will have to be
made in a metal workshop.
Use: For rose arches, gateway
arches, bowers, and covered
walks; for annual and perennial
climbing plants, plants with
tendrils and ramblers.
Securing: This should be carried
out by the manufacturer.

Planting containers

Fortunately, many climbing plants
do not make great demands with
respect to space, so they will
flourish just as well in large
containers, pots, and balcony
boxes.
The most important points to
consider when choosing plants
are:
● All containers, no matter what
material they are made of, must
be equipped with drainage holes
so that excess water can run
away. Very few plants can cope
with waterlogging.
● All large plant containers
require a drainage layer (see
illustration, p. 23).
● Containers for climbing plants
must be sufficiently spacious as
the plant will require plenty of
room for the development of its
roots if it is to produce large
amounts of leaves and flowers.
Annuals will make do with an
ordinary balcony box but
perennials require a container that
is at least 12-16 in (30-40 cm)
deep, and wide enough to leave
space for an insulating layer made
of polystyrene (see winter
protection, p. 29).
● Before purchasing any large,
heavy containers, troughs, or
urns, find out the carrying

capacity of your balcony or patio.
Even if the plants themselves are
not that heavy, the weight of the
containers increases dramatically
when filled with wet compost.
Clay containers: The porous
material from which these
containers are made makes an
exchange of air possible among
the roots of the plant and the risk
of waterlogging is also reduced as
excess water can evaporate
through the walls of the vessel.
On the other hand, rapid
evaporation will also cause the
soil to cool quickly around the
roots, which many plants dislike.
Clay pots and containers are not
suitable for overwintering outside.

My tip: Before using them, clay
and terracotta pots should be
soaked in water long enough so
that no more tiny air bubbles are
seen rising to the surface. This
means that the clay is now
saturated with water and, to begin
with at least, chalky deposits will
be avoided. When they do
appear, scrub them off with a
tough scrubbing brush and a
vinegar and water solution (1:4).

Wooden containers:
● Always stand wooden
containers on a base to prevent
the rapid decay of the wood.

*A wire grid
with a wooden
frame*

*Lay the wire mesh on the wooden frame (left), use U-shaped nails to
fix the edge of the wire (center) and hang up the frame using spacers
(right).*

Nasturtiums quickly produce a mass of colorful flowers on a fence.

Black-eyed Susan is a very undemanding summer-flowering plant.

● Wooden containers are subje[ct] to weathering. Make sure they have been painted inside and ou[t] with a plant-friendly wood protection agent (see p. 12).

Plastic containers: The advantages are fairly obvious. They are cheap to buy, long-lasting, and do not weigh much and are, therefore, ideal for balconies and windowsills. They are also practical and easy to clean as the smooth surface will not encourage the growth of algae.

Troughs made of natural ston[e] Usually, no drainage holes have been provided so the container will require a good drainage laye[r] (see p. 24). Carefully choose the position in which you are going [to] keep the trough as its weight wi[ll] prevent it from being moved about too easily.

Plant containers with a water reservoir: Recently, plant containers with inbuilt water reservoirs have become more widely available. The reservoir is at the bottom of the plant container and, depending on the size of the container, can hold u[p] to 2½ gallons (10 liters) of water. Fertilizer can also be introduced this way.

NB: These containers should als[o] be equipped with a properly functioning water-level indicator. Too much water in the container would cause the roots to rot as they would be standing in water all the time. Even when using th[is] method, you will not be able to dispense with watering for more than a few days as plants in larg[e] containers will require lots of water, particularly if they are placed in a sunny position.

Creating greenery

Walls covered in green foliage are not only an aesthetically pleasing adornment of houses and other buildings in towns, they also provide a habitat for birds and other wild creatures. In this way, foliage and flowering plants, grown against a house wall or in pots and containers, can be used to create a natural haven all around the outside of your house.

A green façade

Before buying plants to cover a wall you should give some thought to what you intend to achieve.

Will you wish to influence the direction in which the plants grow or do you not mind which way they climb up the wall? You could choose climbing plants which require climbing frames that merely need fixing to the wall in the right position for the plant to cover the wall with greenery. Or you may wish to let plants with root suckers, which do not require any climbing aids, grow unhindered up a wall.

Do you want the wall to be covered in greenery as soon as possible and up to what height do you wish the plants to climb? Hops and Russian vine, for example, are recommended as fast-growing climbers; ivy and spindleberry (*Euonymus fortunei*) are much slower, at least for the first few years.

If you wish to cover the entire façade with a uniformly dense, green tapestry, the best plants are ivy and Virginia creeper. If, however, you wish only part of the façade to be hidden or even a particular area of it, for example to emphasize the importance of the entrance, clematis, roses, Dutchman's pipe and honeysuckle would be most suitable.

The advantages of greenery on a façade

Houses covered in climbing plants are not only ecologically beneficial, they also profit from many favourable effects created by the woven covering of plants. Plants growing on a wall provide a kind of protective covering for the house.

A habitat for birds and insects: Green façades create new living spaces which offer many creatures shelter and nesting facilities, and also food in the shape of flowers and fruit. In addition to bees, beetles, butterflies, and spiders, birds, and bats will also join the community on the house wall, where both prey and predators will feel at home.

A temperature equalizer: Plants let water evaporate through their leaves. This process leads to a slight cooling in temperature of their immediate surroundings, which is why outdoor seating in many warm countries is often surrounded by climbing plants.

Due to this effect, houses covered in greenery enjoy a more temperate climate. The temperature is lowered slightly in hot summer weather, while the cold of winter is alleviated a little by an evergreen plant covering. The difference in the daytime and night-time temperature is also decreased.

Protection from rain and weather: A thick plant covering will protect a house wall from rain. There is still plenty of ventilation behind the protective covering of leaves, so the wall will not be covered in condensation. Thickly covered house walls will be shielded even from heavy showers.

Increase in humidity: Plants on a house wall lose water through evaporation to the immediate environment without the moisture condensing on the wall.

Damage to the façade

Very often, damage to a house wall is ascribed to climbing plants which are not the culprits at all. Instead, already damaged or damp masonry is responsible for the problems. The reputedly damaging effect of ivy or Virginia creeper on a façade just does not happen so long as the façade was undamaged to begin with as the adhesive pads and roots will not harm sound rendering or cement. Plants with tendrils and adhesive pads, like Virginia creeper, secrete a sticky substance to let them adhere to the wall and this does no damage to the wall. Climbing plants never bore holes or make cracks in walls, they only take advantage of already existing uneven places and cracks. This means that damaged walls should be properly repaired before letting plants climb up them.

15

Grown in a sunny position, a Virginia creeper will produce beautifully colored fall foliage.

How to avoid damage to a façade

● Ivy or Virginia creeper should not be planted right beside wooden walls that require regular painting. Old sheds or garage walls will suit these plants.

● Façades treated with water-repellent paint are not suitable for plants with root suckers. The root suckers of ivy may penetrate the top layer of paint and continue producing roots underneath this. The consequence will be peeling paint.

● Gutters and the surfaces of roofs should not have plants climbing across them. Self-climbing plants on roof surfaces will push their shoots under the roof tiles and even lift them up.

NB: Gutters that are blocked with growing plants will lead to dampness in walls.

The right side of the house

Different plants have different requirements as to position. The section on care (see pp. 39-59) will tell you which side of the house is suitable for which plants.

The south-facing side: This is the ideal position for kiwi fruit, grapevines, or espalier fruit (the south-facing side is too warm for apples) and deciduous climbing plants like wisteria, roses, honeysuckle, or morning glory.

The west-facing side: This is often the side which receives most rain in northern areas, although it also enjoys the full warmth of the afternoon sunshine and can therefore support espalier fruit. A dense, evergreen covering will protect the fruit against heavy rain.

The east-facing side: Here, the morning sun will still provide enough warmth for active growth and this side is also often more protected than the west-facing side. However, late frosts in spring may damage the flowers of espalier fruit on this side, which may mean a lack of fruit later on.

The north-facing side: Here, it is better to plant evergreen plants which cover the whole surface, like ivy. The north-facing side is not suitable for planting espalier fruit.

Decorative design

Deciding to cover your house with greenery will still leave plenty of scope for your own ideas, whether this is the choosing and combining of different plants, the building of suitable climbing aids, or the optimal utilization of existing surfaces.

nbing roses and Virginia creeper.

The fall colors of Virginia creeper.

reen and flowering
lcony

ufficient screen from
ghboring balconies can be
ained with tall-growing
nbing plants like scarlet runner
ans which can be trained on
ple twines or wires (see p. 11).
vays check about attaching
ures with your landlord.)
en and flowering climbing
nts on horizontal wires or
nes will transform your balcony
o a densely covered, flowering
nmer bower. Annual winders
d plants with tendrils are most
table for this and will manage
te well in flower boxes or pots.
arming contrasts can be
ated with a combination of
nbing plants and annual
nmer flowers in a pot.
rennial species (in containers
h a height of at least 14 in/35

cm and a diameter of 12-16 in/30-
40 cm) which need to overwinter
on a balcony, should be hardy.
*Make sure to consider the
following points when
establishing plants on a
balcony:*
● Balconies that are open to
strong winds require protection
from the wind to let young plants
acclimatize themselves; for
example, by using bamboo
matting as a screen.
● Plants on a balcony are more
susceptible to attack by pests
which means more time spent on
care.
● Boxes fixed to the outside of a
balcony railing must be secured
properly.

Doorways and entrances
You can create greenery around
your entrance door with

honeysuckle, Russian vine and
Virginia creeper – sometimes
these plants will end up supplying
a covering of greenery over the
entire façade. The way to set
plants directly into the soil beside
a doorway is shown on page 22.
A green archway above an
entrance doorway, for example in
the garden of a terraced house,
can be covered with roses,
honeysuckle, or clematis. Large
container plants, like bay and box
trees, can look very charming
beside a rather grander doorway.
Climbing plants can also be
trained on frames or taut wires
(see pp. 11 and 12) on both sides
of a doorway, and may be planted
in large containers or boxes. The
entrance to a house may not
always be in a sheltered position,
so only choose plants that are not
too sensitive to wind and weather.

Color around a window

Windows can be transformed into mini-balconies.

● If there is an outside window ledge, you can utilize the depth and width of the embrasure and stand a box on the ledge. Secure it well, so that it cannot tip off!

● Use lightweight boxes as window ledges cannot cope with a great amount of weight.

● Never install window boxes on the side of the house that is most exposed to wind or rain.

● Hardy, perennial climbing plants, like ivy or clematis, may be allowed to cover a façade from a window by using sufficiently insulated window boxes (see winter protection, p. 29). Draw taut wires or twines along the wall beside the window to provide a climbing frame for the plants. These supports should be secured to the wall with wall hooks that have been dowelled in. Make sure to check with your landlord first.

Clematis alpina "Francess Rivis."

Metal drainpipes as supports for climbing plants

If a vertical drainpipe is anchored properly and is a sufficient space out from a wall, it may be used as an ideal support for less hefty winding plants like Dutchman's pipe, hops, black-eyed Susan or scarlet runner beans. Wisteria, for example, should never be allowed to climb up a drainpipe; its yard-long shoots will become woody and tough in time and are quite capable of "strangling" a drainpipe. Very delicate winding plants, on the other hand, will not be able to use such large pipes.

● If no place for planting is available at the foot of a drainpipe, you can create a planting pit (see p. 23) or set the plants (preferably annuals) in a pot or container.

● In order to prevent the shoots from slipping down the smooth surface of a drainpipe to begin with, you may carefully tie the plant to the pipe or draw a hop twine from the ground to the top. **NB:** Remember to cut the plant back so that it cannot block the top of the drainpipe.

My tip: Do not let plants with tendrils and adhesive pads climb up drainpipes and do not plant them near pipes as their adhesive pads tend to create rust spots on metal surfaces.

Plastic drainpipes should not be used for climbers as they will not bear the weight.

Climbers on a patio

A patio will provide plenty of room for a multitude of different combinations of plants.

Large container plants, like oleander, bougainvillea, or hibiscus, will feel particularly at home on a patio on the south-facing side of the house. (Advic on growing plants in large containers is given on pp. 20-9 *Climbing plants* on patios or fences can turn boring party wa or wire fences between adjoinir gardens into a living screen.

● Honeysuckle, clematis, or roses, planted in beds beside patios or along walls, will produ a riot of summer flowers, particularly if planted in a south facing position.

● If you want to hide a patio w or an adjoining wire fence with covering of green foliage even i winter, the best species to plan are ivy or *Euonymus fortunei* which will also flourish on a nor or east-facing patio.

...matis montana "Rubens" is a profusely flowering variety.

...f there is no room on a house
...l, perennial climbing plants can
...grown in a large trough in front
...a patio wall.

...iple builders' steel mesh or
...nes that have been secured to
...l hooks will be sufficient as a
...nbing aid (see p. 12).

...rubs will also provide a
...nderful visual screen beside a
...io or along a fence. Hedge
...ple, lilac, forsythia, or spiraea
... provide cheerful accents with
...ir flowers, fruit, or colorful fall
...age. Most shrubs will require
...nting in open soil on account of
...ir size and the extent of their
...t systems.

...nces

...ou do not have enough room
...a proper hedge, fences
...nstructed of different materials,
...ch as wire or wood, are
...solutely ideal as climbing aids.

Climbing plants will produce
enchanting flowers in the summer
and Virginia creeper will decorate
your fence with a wealth of
wonderful, glowing-red leaves in
the fall.

● Vertical fence posts are ideal
for supporting winding plants like
convolvulus, black-eyed Susan or
morning glory. Any missing
horizontals needed can easily be
added by drawing rope or wires
from post to post.

● Plants with tendrils, like
nasturtium, clematis or sweet
peas, will climb effortlessly on
small-gauge wire fences.

● Using annual plants, you can
create a different look along a
fence every year and also have the
time to provide wooden posts with
a regular protective coat of paint.

● Vigorously growing perennials,
like wisteria or hops, require a
fence height of at least 7-8 ft (2-

2.5 m). The fence must also be
very strong.

● You can find out just how many
plants you will need for the length
of fence, and the proper spacing
of these plants, on pages. 39-59.

● Plantations of shrubs or other
plants along fences not only
provide an attractive visual
screen, they are also high on the
list of ecologically beneficial
improvements: hazelnut, hedge
maple, or cornelian cherry
(*Cornus mas*) provide shelter and
food for birds and small mammals
like hedgehogs or dormice.

NB: Make sure there will be
enough space between your plants
and any neighboring property
when planting beside fences. Find
out how large the plants will grow
when you buy them.

**Covering garbage can
shelters, fuel stores, etc.**
Even such unattractive objects as
these can be use to support plants
if you choose the right ones.

● Virginia creeper will soon
obscure garbage can shelters and
other structures. Ivy will also
cover such ugly eyesores with its
green foliage but will do better in
less sunny positions.

● Instead of going for a complete
covering, you could also stand
plant troughs of summer flowers,
like patience-plants, pinks or
daisies, or climbing plants with
hanging shoots, like Virginia
creeper (*Parthenocissus
quinquefolia*), on top of a garbage
can shelter and thereby improve
its appearance.

Other sites
Even the composting corner of
the garden can be brightened up
as the bars or grid of the
composting container itself can
provide an excellent climbing
frame for plants.

Flowering, climbing plants, like sweet peas or nasturtiums, which will cover a container with their bright flowers in no time at all, will cheer up any dull corner of the garden. Planting soft fruit bushes, such as red/black/whitecurrants or gooseberries, or other low-growing shrubs, like lilac or forsythia, in front of a composting station will also aid the compost to ripen as maturing compost does not like to receive too much direct sunlight.

Position, planting, and care

Your plants will thrive better if you create the best conditions for healthy growth right from the start. In order to do this you will need to know the individual requirements of the plants with respect to position and soil, when and how to plant them, and how to care for them properly. If all of these conditions are met, your plants will flourish and be the envy of all who see them

Shrubs that are ecologically beneficial
barberry (*Berberis vulgaris*)
broom (*Genista tinctoria*)
buckthorn (*Rhamnus catharticus*)*
cornelian cherry (*Cornus mas*)
elder (*Sambucus nigra* and *S. racemosa**)
hedge maple (*Acer campestre*)
Frangula alnus*
hawthorn (*Crataegus crusgalli*)
hazelnut (*Corylus avellana*)
holly (*Ilex aquifolium*)*
hornbeam (*Carpinus betulus*)
juniper (*Juniperus communis*)
privet (*Ligustrum vulgare*)*
Prunus mahaleb
sloe (*Prunus spinosa*)
snowy mespilus (*Amelanchier lamarckii*)
spindleberry (*Euonymus europaea*)*
whitethorn (*Crataegus monogyna*)
willow (*Salix*)

These bushes provide shelter and food for numerous species of birds and small creatures. (*toxic plants)

Planting

The right time to plant
The best time is in spring when the plants will have enough time to form proper roots and to grow well before the first frosts in late fall.
Container plants or plants sold with a rootstock can be planted all year round but will require a great deal of care and attention. High temperatures during the daytime will inhibit growth.

Position
Light: Not all plants have the same requirements with respect to light. Generally, a distinction is made between:
● positions in full sunlight
● semi-shady positions, and
● shady positions.
Examples of climbing plants which require lots of light include roses and wisteria. However, most native American climbing plants normally grow wild in semi-shady positions on the fringes of woodland; for example hops. Ivy is a good shade provider in the wild.
Temperature: Sufficient warmth is essential to the survival of many plants. Sunny, and therefore warm, positions are ideal for fro sensitive plants like woody espalier plants or large containe plants. Flowering climbing plant will also thrive here. Evergreen climbing plants prefer positions with a more balanced temperat (even north-facing).
Soil: Depending on their requirements, individual plants thrive in various different kinds soil. Even if the soil has been improved (see p. 22), you shou not try to grow plants that requ a rich soil in a very poor one.
Water: Most climbing plants require a plentiful supply of wat to help them to absorb the nutrients in the soil.

Planting in open soil
The work involved in planting a care is less involved if you plant directly into open soil as, here, climbing plants will find the kinc conditions that most closely resemble those of their natural habitat:
● They are growing directly in soil, so they have plenty of spa for their roots to grow.
● They will be supplied with plenty of rainwater.

a patio

ending on the site of the
, you may have to provide
ection from the wind in order
otain a really sheltered
tion for Mediterranean plants
spalier fruit trees. As most
os are situated on the south
of the house, the plants
ted or kept there are subject
tense sunlight and
siderable differences in
erature during the course of
day. More watering by the
ener will therefore be needed
for plants planted in open
(see p. 26).

soil in beds along the sides of
patios is often mixed with
ders' rubble and will have to
proved before you plant
hing (see p. 22).

a balcony

onies share many features of
tio but the amount of light
ived may be impaired by
hboring balconies or shadows
ted by other nearby buildings.
ng the summer, balconies
turn into real heat traps for
ts, as heat reflected from road
aces or house walls may
ct there. It is, therefore,
icularly important to provide
able shading and to water the
ts adequately (see p. 26).
t to watch out for when
ting in balcony boxes is
ained on page.24.

Virginia creeper will provide a protective covering for your house.

Planting beside walls

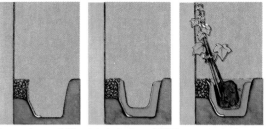

Dig a planting hole, lay a piece of filter fabric in it and fill the space between the hole and the wall with gravel. Mix dug-out soil with improving substances. Insert the plant, lean the support stick against the wall, and fill up the hole with soil.

Types of soil and how to improve them

As a rule, climbing plants demand fairly loose, nutrient-rich soil such as humus-rich garden soil. As most soils do not possess all the features of an ideal plant soil, they have to be improved with loosening or binding substances and should receive basic fertilization before planting commences (see p.28).

Sandy soils generally contain very little humus.
● Characteristics: A fine, crumbly structure, therefore very water-permeable and easy for roots to penetrate, but with a decreased capacity for storing nutrients.
● Improvement: Use organic fertilizers and binding substances like loam and organic compost.

Loamy soils often contain plenty of humus.
● Characteristics: If there is a high clay content, it may be difficult for roots to penetrate. A loamy soil should have a good capacity for retaining nutrients. If it dries out severely, large cracks may cause damage to roots.
● Improvement: Use sand for loosening and compost or stable manure as fertilizer to turn it into an ideal growing medium.

Chalky soils, depending on their situation, will naturally tend to contain a thin or thicker layer of humus.
● Characteristics: Usually lumpy or gravelly so very permeable for water and nutrients.
● Improvement: Use sand and compost for loosening, and stable manure and mineral fertilizers for fertilizing.

Peaty or marshy soils will have either a thin or thick layer of humus on top.
● Characteristics: As a rule, poor in nutrients, loose and easy for roots to penetrate when drained; not a good growing medium.
● Improvement: Add mineral fertilizers and lime.

Soil exchange: An exchange of soil is necessary if climbing plants are to be planted beside a wall where soil is often full of builders' rubble or is very compact (very difficult for roots to penetrate). In some cases, you may even have to remove flagstones, tiles, or similar coverings beforehand. Unwanted material like chunks of concrete, stone chippings, or coarse gravel, should be completely removed. The remaining soil should be improved with humus, fertilizer (mineral or organic, see. p. 27), and, depending on the type of soil, with loosening or binding substances.

Compost for plants in large containers and boxes

Plants which have to make do with small volumes of soil or compost must be supplied with compost that is adapted to their requirements.

Ripe garden compost is very rich in nutrients and very suitable for growing plants. It can be taken as waste matter from a kitchen garden or made from vegetable and plant kitchen scraps etc. in a compost heap in your own garden. You can buy special composting bins in garden centers.

Suitable growing mediums are also sold as ready-to-use products in garden centers etc.

Standard compost, which is sold in bags, usually consists of loam soil and peat. Often, loosening substances like polystyrene fragments and fertilizer are mixed in with it so that this compost can be used for planting without further preparation.

Peat consists of the dead parts of marginal plants. Due to its very fibrous structure, peat acts as a loosening agent in compost and soil. It absorbs and stores water well and is contained in many commercial composts.

Despite this, environmentally aware gardeners are now recommended to avoid using peat as much as possible as producing it contributes to the destruction and loss of large areas of natural wetlands and moors.

Ordinary garden soil is rarely suitable for large containers. Depending on its consistency, soil-improving substances will probably have to be added to it.

Pruning

Climbing plants which can be bought in tree nurseries and are sold with roots but without soil around them, should be cut bac

nediately before planting. The
ove-ground shoots should be
 back by about one-third of
ir length, and the roots by
out ½-¾ in (1-2 cm).
maged roots or those that
re obviously dried up should
cut back to where they look
althy. Thicker main roots (more
n a finger-wide) should be left.
ntainer plants should not have
ir roots cut back and the
oots should be pruned only
ringly as plants with a properly
ered rootstock should not
fer shock from being replanted.
rubs and annual climbing
nts that are almost exclusively
ainable as container plants
uld not be cut back before
nting.

e correct way to plant

 way a plant is planted affects
 way it will grow. It is, therefore,
ticularly important to observe a
 basic rules when planting in a
ll-prepared position so that the
nt is sure to thrive.

nting in open soil

en preparing a planting hole,
 should check, even before
ving the plant, that the soil is
se, easy for roots to penetrate
 not too sandy. A small "trial
e" of about two spades' depth
 be dug to check this point. If
 soil is too stony or contains
 much clay, you can buy the
cessary improving substances
he same time as the plant (see
22). Exchanging the soil later
 after planting, is both difficult
 usually harmful to the plant.
: The size of the planting hole
pends on the size of the
tstock which should have
ugh room in the hole to
and. As a general rule, be

guided by the standard
dimensions of 24 by 24 by 24 in
(60 by 60 by 60 cm).

Method
● Dig the planting hole.
● When digging, make sure that
the darker soil on top is not mixed
with the lighter soil underneath; if
possible, pile them up separately.
● The bottom of the planting hole
should be loosened up with a
spade, shovel or a pick, to a
depth of at least 8 in (20 cm).
● Carefully remove the plant from
its container, stand it in the planting
hole and check the position.
● Take the plant out again and
place some of the lighter
undersoil, mixed with soil-
improvement substances or
compost (mixing ratio 1:1), in the
hole so that, when placed in the
hole, the neck of the root of the
plant will be level with the top
edge of the hole.
● If the plants have been bought
with the rootstock tied in a
covering such as sacking, make
sure you loosen the cloth at the
neck and remove any tight twines.
The cloth should remain around
the roots as it will decay in time.
● Now, shovel in the rest of the
dark topsoil, mixed with
controlled-release fertilizer (hoof
and horn chips or mineral

fertilizer, see p. 27), making sure
that you follow the manufacturer's
directions. Place this around the
plant and tread it down firmly.
● Use the remaining soil to create
a shallow gulley around the plant
for watering purposes.

Care after planting
● Water the plants well (about 1¼-
2½ gallons/5-10 liters or more,
depending on the size of the plant).
● Self-climbing plants should be
trained toward the wall using the
stick to which the young plant was
tied when bought, in order to give
the plant some hold (see p. 22).
● Remove the support sticks of
plants with tendrils and winding
plants and immediately tie the
plant to the climbing aid which
you have already installed.
● After watering, protect the
planting area from drying out by
mulching (using straw, grass
cuttings, or bark mulch). This will
also prevent the growth of weeds.

Planting directly beside a wall
If the planting area is right beside a
house or garage wall that would be
damaged by moisture or water
splashes, the wall should be given
a coat of insulating paint. If this
cannot be done, a layer of gravel,
approximately 16 in (40 cm) wide
(see p. 22), should be laid between
the wall and the planting area.

*Drainage in a
large container*

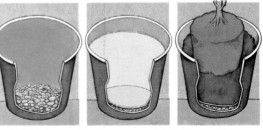

*Place a 2-4-in (5-10-cm) thick layer of drainage material in the container.
Lay filter fabric on top and draw it up to the inside edge of the container.
Add the compost. Stand the plant in the container, shovel in compost
between the pot and the rootstock, and press down firmly. Water well.*

Spindleberry.

Clematis hybrid.

Honeysuckle.

You will require: gravel (⅔ in/16 mm in diameter) and filtering fabric.

Method
● To protect the wall, dig a trench 12-16 in (30-40 cm) wide and 8 in (20 cm) deep along it.
● Dig out the actual planting area adjacent to it (approx. 24 in/60 cm wide and 24 in/60 cm deep). Then treat the dug out soil in the same way as when planting in open soil (see p. 23).
● Fill the shallow pit along the wall with a layer of gravel.
● Lay the filtering fabric between the gravel and the planting area.
● Insert the plant and then fill up the planting area with soil.
NB: All work carried out outside the boundaries of your property will require permission from your local council or neighbor.

Planting in large containers and boxes
When choosing the height of the container, consider the eventual height of the plant and the size of its rootstock. The plant will need enough space for its roots to spread out and should not be squeezed into its container.
NB: To give protection against freezing in winter, an insulating liner should be placed in the container before inserting the drainage layer (see p. 29).
Drainage: To prevent waterlogging or a blockage of the drainage holes, before planting, larger containers should first be filled with a 2-4 in (5-10 cm) layer of gravel (of about ⅓⅔ in/8-16 mm diameter) or with Hortag. Hortag is much lighter than gravel and is therefore ideal for large plant containers. Cover the

drainage holes with broken piec of pot beforehand. Over the drainage layer spread a layer of fabric filter which should then be pulled up around the sides to th top edge of the container. This will prevent compost or soil bein washed down the sides of the fabric and into the drainage laye
Planting
● After planting, carefully water the plant but do not flood it.
● It is better to water several times sparingly on a daily basis.
● If the planting medium has sunk down a little after a few days, top up the container with extra compost and form a watering gulley (see p. 23).
● Do not fertilize plants bought garden centers until about six weeks after planting, as they wil already have been provided with controlled-release fertilizer.

Morning glory and ornamental gourd.

Russian vine.

Climbing rose.

Plants from other sources can have controlled-release fertilizer mixed in with their compost. Once you have done this, do not fertilize again for another four weeks.
Balcony boxes with summer flowers planted in them will not require a drainage layer as they are not very deep. They should, however, still have drainage holes which should be covered with fragments of broken pot.
● An ordinary balcony box that is only 4¾ in (12 cm) wide, 6 in (15 cm) deep will be too small for perennial climbing plants. They require containers with a capacity of 7½-10 gallons (30-40 liters).
● Annual climbing plants, on the other hand, will manage in standard-size balcony boxes (see pp. 26 and 27) as long as they are given the right amount of water and fertilizer.

● Adequate protection from frost (see p. 29) will also be necessary for balcony boxes if the plants are expected to overwinter in them.

Planting annual climbing plants
Annuals that are pre-grown in pots or large containers often have a headstart with respect to growth but, having begun life in a greenhouse, are also often more sensitive than hardened, home-grown plants.
Sowing and raising: The seed of many climbing plants can be bought or collected and sown in pots (larger seeds) or seed trays. The seed compost in the seed tray should be moistened slightly (use a spray bottle) and the tray should be covered with a transparent lid or plastic wrap. Also cover pots with plastic wrap.

From time to time, lift the film or lid for ventilation.
Pots or seed trays should be placed in a warm, light but not too bright spot; the seeds require a temperature of about 68°F (20°C) to germinate. During this time, keep the surface of the seed compost slightly moist. The germinating seeds are usually too densely packed in a tray to develop fully. The tiny plantlets have to be thinned out to provide more space when two germ leaves are fully developed. The space between rows should be 4 in (10 cm) and the spaces between individual plants 2 in (5 cm) (see illustration, p. 26).
Sowing in open soil: You can obtain the seeds of many annual climbing plants from garden centers. These can be sown straight into open soil.

Particularly robust species, like scarlet runner beans, nasturtiums, and convolvulus, are well suited to this method:

● Soak larger seeds in lukewarm water overnight to speed up germination.

● Make a 2-in (5-cm) deep drill in loose garden soil (for several plants growing beside each other) or a 2-in (5-cm) deep hole for each seed (check the directions for depth on the package).

● Lay the seeds in the hole (if there are several, ensure correct spacing which should be indicated on the package, probably three to five seeds) and cover them with soil.

● The seeds will germinate sooner if you lay a piece of plastic sheeting over the planting area, weighted down with stones around the edges. When the seedlings appear, the sheet can be removed or raised on wooden or wire sticks so that the plants have room to grow. It is advisable not to plant seeds before the last cold snap toward the middle of the last month of spring as the young plants will not cope with frost.

Planting in open soil: Annual climbing plants have very special soil requirements because of their rapid growth and they also require a good supply of nutrients. The hole should be dug as described on page 23. However, a hole with a depth of 12 in (30 cm) will be sufficient.

Planting in large containers and boxes: If your home-grown or bought annual climbing plants are to be planted in a large container or balcony box, proceed as for planting in large containers (see p. 24).

Sowing seed in a seed tray and pricking out
Sow the seed evenly, using a folded piece of paper. Cover the seed tray with plastic wrap. Loosen the seedlings from the growing medium with the thin end of a pricking-out tool. Make a hole with the thick end of the pricking-out tool and plant the seedling deep enough for the first leaves to lie on the surface of the growing medium. Press down lightly.

Care

If you know what a plant's requirements are, you can ensure that it has the best possible care. Every plant has to be supplied with an adequate amount of water and nutrients. There are also other measures of care to attend to for climbing plants, such as tying up shoots, the occasional pruning, and, if necessary, providing protection against cold and frost. Plants which are not growing in open soil, but are planted in large containers or boxes, are particularly dependent on regular and sometimes intensive care.

Watering

Water is essential for all plants. The amount of water that plants lose daily through evaporation from their leaves depends on the temperature on that day, the humidity, and the amount of direct sunlight. The following rule applies: the cooler the day and the higher the humidity, the less water the plants will require.

NB: Do not water plants during midday or in intense direct sunlight.

Plants in open soil need not be watered quite as often as plants in large containers or boxes on account of their widely spreading root systems.

● It is important that you water thoroughly so that even the deepest roots are adequately supplied with moisture.

● Young or recently planted plants need more frequent watering. For the rest, it will be sufficient to water every eight to ten days during the main growth period (from the second month of spring to the second month of fall).

● Annual climbing plants that are situated in a sunny position should be watered more often.

● During the winter, water evergreen climbing plants like ivy only occasionally and only on frost-free days.

Plants in large containers and boxes, which contain relatively little compost, will use up water rapidly.

How often you water will depend on the individual requirements of plants, the size of the planting container, and on the weather. The basic rule is:

● Plants in pots should be watered more often than those growing in open soil.

● Large, vigorously growing plants in pots require more frequent watering as the supply of water in the rootstock will be used up more quickly.

● On hot summer days, water plants growing on a patio or balcony twice daily, preferably in the morning and evening.

● Consider what type of containers the plants are in: water will not evaporate quite so quickly from plastic containers as from clay containers.

● You can usually tell by looking at the leaves whether plants need water: if they are drooping or the leaves are rolled up, they are in desperate need of water.

The "finger test" will determine whether a plant is thirsty. Push a finger about ½ in (1 cm) deep into the top of the compost. If it feels damp, you will not need to water that day; if it feels dry, water well.

Rainwater is still to be recommended for watering, despite the increase in pollution, and is still better for plants than hard, lime-rich main water. Main water should be left to stand for a few days before using it.

Watering during holidays: Watering large container or balcony plants can be a problem if you are to be away from home for any length of time. Irrigation systems are sold in garden centers but you should always test these thoroughly before you go away to make sure that they work properly. If you are going away for a brief vacation, you should be able to manage by using plant containers with inbuilt water reservoirs (see p. 14). The most reliable "system," however, is still a friend or accommodating neighbor who will follow your written instructions!

My tip: Watering balcony boxes that are attached to the outside of a balcony railing may cause inconvenience to neighbors with balconies under yours. If you do not have very tolerant neighbors below you, it is better to hang the boxes on the inside of the railing.

Fertilizing

Plants require certain nutrients for growth and well-being. Particularly during the vegetative period, while the plant is growing and flowering, it should be provided with sufficient nutrients. Nutrients that are lacking in the soil or compost must be replaced and this is done by fertilizing. Some species like a lot of fertilizer, such as scarlet runner beans or ornamental gourds, while other, less demanding, plants, such as wild forms of clematis and ivy, manage on very little.

The frequency of fertilizing during the growth period depends on the individual plant species and is described in the instructions for care (see pp. 39-59).

Types of fertilizer: Fertilizers are available in solid, dried or liquid form.

● Liquid fertilizers do not need to be dissolved in water first and are particularly suitable for plants in large containers or on balconies.

● Solid fertilizers are mixed with the soil or compost and will gradually release nutrients to the plant as these nutrients must first be broken down through the action of water.

The nutrient composition of fertilizers: In addition to the three main nutrients of nitrogen (N), phosphorus (P), and potassium (K), plants also need lesser quantities of trace elements like magnesium, iron, sulphur, copper, boron, and manganese.

● Nitrogen supports the upward growth of plants and the development of leaves. Nitrogen deficiency is recognizable by yellow leaves and stunted growth.

● Phosphorus is necessary for the formation of roots, flowers, and fruit.

● Potassium builds up the plant's resistance to disease and pests.

Compound fertilizer (mineral and inorganic fertilizer) contains all of the main nutrients. However, the nutrient composition is not the same for all fertilizers. The proportions of main nutrients in any fertilizer are always expressed as the abbreviation N P K, and given as a ratio in that order on the outside of the packaging. Thus, 7:7:7 means equal proportions of nitrogen, phosphorus and potassium are included, each nutrient comprising 7 percent of the total content.

NB: 2 tablespoons (20 g) mineral fertilizer per 40 sq in (1 sq m) is enough.

Types of fertilizer

● Mineral fertilizers or inorganic fertilizers contain nutrients in the form of soluble salts. When given to the plant as granules, they are dissolved by water and washed down among the roots. Controlled-release fertilizer contains nutrients in the form of small beads which release the nutrients very gradually aided by the action of moisture.

● Organic (or biological) fertilizers consist of animal products like ground hoof and horn, horn chips, dried blood, animal dung, or plant extracts. This type of fertilizer often provides only one nutrient: animal manure and horn chips, for example, provide nitrogen; bonemeal provides phosphorus. Organic fertilizers are generally not compound fertilizers and it takes a relatively long time for the nutrients to become effective.

An attractive visual screen – a wire fence covered with ivy and Virginia creeper.

How often to fertilize

Plants growing in open soil need not be fertilized quite so often as plants in large containers or boxes, as they can draw on a natural reservoir of soil nutrients. Large container plants and balcony plants have to be supplied with fertilizer on a regular basis in order to balance the disadvantages created by their positions.

● One or two doses of fertilizer will be sufficient for perennial climbing plants during the vegetation period.

● Annual climbing plants that are growing in open soil require regular fertilizing at intervals of about four to six weeks over their short growing period.

● A weekly dose of fertilizer is recommended for plants in smaller containers or pots; fertilizing every two weeks will be sufficient for larger containers (from 12-16 in/30-40 cm high).

● Large container plants should not be fertilized after the end of summer so that they can prepare themselves for winter.

As a basic fertilizer for woody plants: mix the main nutrients NPK (ratio 10:10:15) with the planting medium if you are not using compost that already contains fertilizer.

Plants sold with a rootstock, or container plants, will welcome a starter boost from an organic fertilizer. Plants in pots should be fertilized again about six to eight weeks after planting. Plants in open soil should be fertilized about two to three months after planting.

The right way to fertilize

● Only provide fertilizer if the plant is able to absorb nutrients; that is, during the growth phase from spring to fall.

● Always read the manufacturer's directions regarding dosage.

● Never strew the fertilizer on dry soil or compost as the roots would soon suffer burns from such a high concentration of nutrients.

● Always mix controlled-release fertilizer with the soil or compost.

Mistakes in fertilizing

● Signs of a lack of fertilizer: Meager growth, lack of flowers, light-colored or discolored leaves. An immediate dose of compound fertilizer will help, preferably in liquid form.

● Signs of an excess of fertilizer: Brown spots on leaves or burned edges to leaves, unnaturally long shoots, very large, limp leaves. Remedy: In the case of potted plants, thoroughly drench the area of the roots in running water. This is best done in a bath. Do not water the plant again for about three days. In the case of plants growing in open soil, all you can do is water very thoroughly.

Tying up

It is sometimes necessary to tie parts of climbing plants to a support as, occasionally, the plants will not manage to find the support provided on their own or will simply send their shoots out in another direction.

Even self-climbers like ivy or Virginia creeper are grateful for initial help in training them toward a wall or fence.

Ramblers, like climbing roses, will need to have their new shoots tied up regularly.

In the case of espalier fruit, tying up is very important as it serves to anchor the new growth, determines the direction in which

the plant will continue to grow and stimulates fruit production (see tying up espaliers, p. 32).

Plant-friendly tying materials include garden twine, hemp string, or rope and rubberized wire.

NB: When tying up plants, give consideration to the potential thickness of the shoots; the tie should not be too tight around the shoot as this will interfere with transportation of water and nutrients and the outer skin of the shoot may be rubbed raw or damaged. The best way to proceed is to make a loose loop around the shoot, tie a second loop around the support stick etc., and then finish off this loop with a knot, making a figure of eight.

Pruning

Generally speaking, climbing plants do not require much pruning but will cope with it quite well as a rule. Otherwise, only frost-damaged shoots need cutting back to green, healthy wood in the spring.

Winter protection

By late fall sufficient winter protection should be provided against severe frost. The first step toward this is made by choosing hardy plants in the first place and then planting them in the right position, for example somewhere sheltered.

Frost protection in open soil: It is mainly young plants that are at risk here but roses and warmth-loving climbing plants will also be very grateful for some form of protection when the temperature drops below zero.

How to protect your plants

● Heaping up soil around the stem, to a height of 8-12 in (20-30 cm), and covering this with

brushwood, straw, or conifer branches (also to a height of 8-12 in/20-30 cm) will protect the plants from freezing to death.

● Climbing roses or more sensitive climbing plants like wisteria can also be wrapped in bundles of straw or brushwood along the length of their longer shoots.

● In the case of evergreen climbing plants, frost damage can be avoided by watering the plants during the fall and on frost-free days in winter. Lack of water will increase susceptibility to damage.

Frost protection for plant containers: If you wish to overwinter perennial climbers in large containers on a balcony or patio, you will have to provide adequate insulation of the containers against frost.

Method

● Before planting or inserting a drainage layer (see p. 24), line the inside walls of the container with ¼-½-in (5-10-mm) thick polystyrene sheeting. The drainage layer will protect the floor of the container against freezing.

● If the container is round, draw the filter fabric up to about 2 in (5 cm) below the upper edge of the container and insert a ½-¾-in (1-2-cm) layer of coarse sand or grit between the wall of the container and the layer of fabric.

● Always choose containers that are frost-proof for overwintering outside (see p. 13).

● Cover plants in large containers with brushwood or straw.

NB: Large container plants, for example oleander or fuchsia, cannot be overwintered outside and will require particular conditions in their winter quarters, so it is important to find out about any such requirements before you purchase sensitive plants in order to avoid disappointment later.

Fruit espaliers

One of the reasons why espaliers are so popular is their dual blessing of attractive foliage and a harvest of fruit. Espalier fruit trees bear enchanting blossoms and you can also fulfil your ambition of picking fresh pears, apples, peaches, or apricots straight from your own house wall. Some most decorative forms of espalier can be created, even by novice gardeners.

Points to note about fruit espaliers

The difference between espalier fruit trees and fruit trees grown in open soil is that an artificial shape of growth is produced by tying up and judicious pruning. This makes it possible to produce tasty, fully ripened fruit in a small space, for example on a house or garage wall.

Growing aids for espaliers

There are various different possibilities for growing espalier fruit on a wall. All methods involve directing the shoots into the desired shape by fixing them to a growing aid. The following are suitable growing aids:

● Wooden frames made of battens or sticks (see p. 12).
● Horizontally and/or vertically stretched wires (depending on the shape of the espalier) which have to be fixed to the wall with the aid of dowelled wall hooks.
● Horizontal wires drawn tautly between two wooden posts which are about 3-4 in (8-10 cm) thick. At each end of the planting area you should drive the wooden posts into the soil slightly at an angle and at least 28 in (70 cm) deep. Depending on the height of

the espalier, the posts may protrude up to 7 ft (2 m) above the soil.
NB: All growing aids should be a minimum distance of 4-12 in (10-30 cm) from the house wall (see p. 11) and should be erected and fixed to the wall before planting.

Shapes of espaliers
These fruit-bearing woody plants can be used to enhance a façade in many different forms. Both stems and branches can be trained into geometric shapes. The average height of growth of individual plants is important in determining the final shape of the espalier; vigorously growing varieties, such as pears, for example, can be trained to cover an entire house wall with greenery.
The most commonly seen espalier shapes are:
● A cordon which is the simplest espalier shape. It consists of a vertical stem or trunk without any lateral branches and is, therefore, very suitable for narrow spaces, for example between a door and a window. The distance between two such trees should be no less than 20-24 in (50-60 cm); only plant varieties with similar speeds of growth beside each other.

● A U-shape, which forms a "double" cordon without a continuous main shoot. The space between individual branches should be 24-32 in (60-80 cm) (see p. 31).
● A palmette with a broad fan shape and much branching; this is particularly suitable for vigorously growing varieties in larger areas (see p. 31).
● A high espalier, for which a long, vertical stem is first grown and lateral branching is allowed to begin at a certain height (for example around windows on the ground floor). This shape may grow right up to the gable of a house and is often used for vigorously growing pear trees.
NB: When choosing the shape of an espalier you must always consider the speed and final extent of growth of the fruit tree.

Suitable fruit species
Species suitable for planting as espaliers are: apples, pears, peaches, apricots, and grapevines. Growing fruit against a house wall in this way brings the benefit of extra warmth, so that, even in regions with a rougher climate, gardeners can still grow their own fruit.
Information about the positioning and care of the espalier fruit varieties mentioned here can be found on pages 56-59.

Planting and care of espalier fruit trees

Fruit grown on espaliers requires more intensive care than that given to perennial climbing plants in open soil: in addition to fertilizing and watering, careful pruning and regular tying up are essential if you want to obtain a worthwhile harvest.

The best position

Fruit growing requires special climatic conditions. Before you decide on the varieties you intend to buy, do make a realistic assessment of your normal climate and temperature. If you give this information to the nursery from which you are ordering plants, their expert staff will be able to advise you if your choice is unsuitable and suggest alternatives.

A house wall that you intend to use for growing espalier fruit should meet the following requirements:

● The wall should be situated in a sheltered position, as draughts will prevent the plant from benefiting from accumulated warmth.

● It should be well ventilated; that is, there must be adequate space between the wall and the espalier.

● The more sun that reaches the wall, the more demanding the types of fruit you can try to grow on it.

The best side of the house for establishing an espalier is the south-facing one. Even in unfavorable regions (high altitude, areas affected by late frosts), you can often plant particularly warmth-loving varieties of fruit, such as peaches, apricots, or late-ripening varieties, against a south-facing wall.

Planting them too close together may cause the plants to be harmed by temperatures that become too high. Insufficient ventilation between the wall and the espalier will encourage fungal infection, such as mildew, in many fruit varieties (see p. 35).

NB: Many house walls are not adequately protected against the water splashes and rising damp that may penetrate from the adjoining planting area (see planting against walls, p. 23).

The right soil

In many cases, the soil immediately in front of a wall is not suitable for growing espalier fruit unless it has been adequately prepared beforehand. Large items such as tiles, flagstones, asphalt, etc., will have to be removed before planting and the soil underneath must be replaced with suitable soil (see p. 22). The length of the planting hole will depend on the desired width of the espalier, but the minimum depth and width of the hole should not be less than 40 in (1 m).

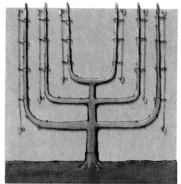

Palmette
This shape can be created with four, six, or more arms. Never choose an uneven number of branches for this palmette as the tree will look unbalanced.

As a rule, *fruit trees* prefer a warm, permeable, crumbly, moist soil. In addition to these characteristics, the right nutrient content is also of great importance (see p. 32). Pure humus soils or garden soils are usually deficient in minerals. By mixing in the right fertilizers, both the nutrient content and the mineral content can be improved (see soil improvement, p. 22).

NB: Information on the soil requirements of popular espalier fruits can be found on pages 56-59.

The correct way to plant

Espalier fruit should be pruned immediately before planting, when all branches should be cut back by about one-third of their length. Before planting, also cut back the fine roots slightly, thereby encouraging renewed root formation. When planting espalier fruit, you should note the following points:

● Soak the rootstock of the young tree in a bucket before planting.

A U-shaped fruit espalier

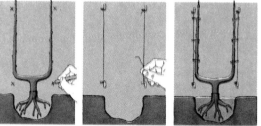

Stand the espalier tree in the planting hole and mark the positions for the wall hooks on the wall. Take the tree out, fix the hooks to the wall, and draw wires between them (corresponding to the shape of the espalier). Insert the tree in the hole. Tie the little tree to the growing aid. Check the ties from time to time to make sure they are not too tight or loose.

Planting trees

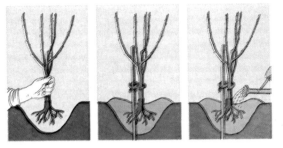

Stand the young tree in the prepared planting hole. Fill the hole with soil and tie the tree to a wooden support stick. The grafting point should end up about a hand span above the soil. Make a gulley for watering and water the young tree well.

● Dig out the planting hole (see planting in open soil, p. 23), loosen the soil well, and fill the hole again, to about two-thirds, with soil.

● Drive a wooden stake into the soil as a support for the young tree (diameter 3-5 in/8-10 cm).

● Stand the young tree in the planting hole, shovel in the rest of the soil, and tread it down firmly all around the tree.

● The grafting point (recognizable as a lump at the lower end of the stem) must remain above the soil or roots will start forming from it that will grow into unwelcome wild shoots which will draw energy and nutrients from the grafted fruit variety.

● Tie the young tree to the support stake using a figure of eight loop made of coconut fiber or hemp twine, and then nail the tie to the post so it cannot slip down.

● Leave a gulley for watering around the tree (see p. 23) and water well.

● Tie the shoots of the young tree to the growing aid in the desired shape.

Fertilizing espalier fruit
A soil containing a balanced ratio of organic and mineral nutrients is an important precondition for the healthy development of an espalier tree.

Nitrogen will encourage the roots to develop and shoots to grow. If too much nitrogen is supplied, however, the trees will become susceptible to disease and the fruit will rapidly decay.

Phosphorus encourages the formation of fruit and the ripening process and ensures a good flavor.

Potassium strengthens the plant and is important for good wood and fruit formation.

How often to fertilize
Fertilizer mixed in with the soil at the time of planting will last for the first year. Well-established espalier fruit trees should be fertilized two or three times a year; the best times are in the spring when the plant starts growing again and after the harvest, around the time when the wood ripens, to encourage resistance against frost.

Espalier fruit trees like fertilizer such as:
● well-rotted manure
● compound fertilizer (see p. 27)
● garden compost that is

mixed with organic fertilizer.

● In addition to compost or compound fertilizer, you should also give the plants fermented plant brews in the spring and fall. A combination of fermented nettle and borage brew (see p. 37) acts as both a fertilizer and an effective plant protection agent.

NB: Avoid unripened, fresh manure as this can burn the roots.

Water sparingly, but regularly
The area around the plant should be kept fairly moist, although fruit trees do not like "wet feet." Waterlogging in the area of the roots may cause fruit trees to die off.

NB: When fruit espaliers are grown against very sunny walls, you may have to water twice on very hot summer days.

A short-term period of dryness will not damage espalier fruit unduly.

Tying espaliers
Tying performs several functions in the case of espalier fruit. It serves to:
● fasten the shoots to the climbing aid
● train the shoots in the desired direction of growth
● encourage fruit formation.

Tying horizontally encourages the food made by the leaves through photosynthesis to be stored in the flower buds and thereby aids fruit formation. (Vertical shoots tend to produce leaves rather than buds.)

When trained horizontally, espaliers require less pruning as fewer vertical shoots are formed. The general rule is to cut less and tie up more.

How to train for horizontal growth:
Humidity makes wood more

le, so the best time to tie up
ches is in the morning or
ing.
rsuading the first branches
young fruit tree to grow in a
ontal plane without breaking
ade easier by hanging small
l tags or clay pots on them
on with twine around the
le of the branch). The
ches will gradually be pulled
n by the weight.
uitable materials for tying are
en twine, hemp string,
kage string, or even coconut
rope for larger branches.
he branches should be tied to
growing frame by means of
e figure-of-eight loops.
The branches should not end
rooping downward but
uld be more or less horizontal.

fting fruit varieties
rule, espalier fruit trees are
ted onto the stock of another
tree, sometimes even on-to
her fruit species. Grafting
es it possible to combine very
rent qualities of two varieties
uit, for example combining a
d yield with hardiness to frost
esistance against fungal
ctions and a prolific formation
uit or larger fruit. The grafting
t is generally thicker than the
of the stem on account of the
a tissue that has formed at the
t of cutting. It may be either
ctly above the neck of the root
n the case of quince or cherry)
he upper end of the stem just
w the branches. The grafting
uit varieties is carried out in
cialist nurseries. If you wish to
w more about it, you can
ain information from your local
dening society or plant nursery.
igorous stock grown from a
dling has the following
antages: it is robust and
demanding; it is suitable for

positions where the soil quality is
not very good or the climate is
rough; it is recommended for wall
espaliers, especially high ones.
A less vigorously growing stock
is better suited to smaller areas,
for example between windows.
NB: Before buying any fruit tree
for training into an espalier, you
should find out from the nursery
whether the stock and the
espalier shape you are planning to
grow are suited to each other.

Pruning espalier fruit trees

It is not possible within the limited
scope of this book to cover the
various methods of pruning in
great detail and you would be well
advised to consult other,
specialist literature on this subject
(inquire at your local library or
garden center). I have, however,
included a few basic pieces of
information.

When to prune
There are many different opinions
on this matter. However, the
following basic rule can be applied:
*The main time for pruning is in
early spring* when the tree has
hardly any foliage. At any other
time severe pruning carries a risk

Thinning out cut
*The old and infertile shoots are
removed (see marked cutting
points, left) so that light and air will
be able to penetrate the crown.*

of the tree being badly debilitated
or even killed through loss of sap.
Spring pruning can include
removing branches and shoot tips
that died during the winter.
Pruning is also simpler at this time
as the fruit and leaf buds are
better formed and therefore more
easily seen.
General rule: Fruit buds are
usually larger than leaf buds. If
you cannot distinguish them, ask
an expert to identify them for you
the first time or else simply decide
for yourself and wait to see what
appears when the bud opens.
Fall is also a time for pruning
espalier fruit trees. Do not do this
too early, however, as the trees will
still be producing too much sap
and the wood will not have
matured. Ripe wood will survive
the winter better. (A sign of ripened
wood is when the leaves start to
discolor and finally fall off.)

My tip: Prune your trees again
after the harvest is over as this will
strengthen them.

For pruning you will need a
strong pair of secateurs, a
wound-sealing substance, a small
saw, and a sharp, preferably
slightly curved, knife.
NB: The secateurs should be your
main tool when pruning. If you
have to start sawing away, it
usually indicates that you have
previously neglected a few
necessary duties. Remember that
it is better to prune more often
and cut away less each time.
Tips on pruning
● Mark the branches with colored
wax crayon before cutting as this
will help you to take off the right
branches.
● Cut the branches off straight,
using secateurs. Any ragged or
frayed cuts should be cut cleanly
with a sharp knife afterwards.

● Cut surfaces that are larger than 1¼ in (3 cm) in diameter should be treated with a wound-sealing substance to encourage growth of new tissue and to prevent the secretion of sap.
● If a large branch is cut right beside the main stem or taken from the crown, make sure that no stumps remain to create a risk of invasion by fungal infection.

Training cut

This can be used to give your espalier tree the right shape of crown during its first year, as this will be determined by the main shoots. As the espalier is basically a flattened shape, you should let only lateral branches remain as main shoots in order to create the correct shape; all other shoots should be cut back to the stem and the cut surfaces treated with a wound sealant. Weaker shoots and those that tend to the vertical should be removed during the training cut. Only the main shoots which will produce the branches that will bear the fruit should be left.

A thinning-out cut

A thinning-out cut should be undertaken in fruit trees for the following reasons:
● To provide the crown with sufficient light and ventilation.
● To maintain a balance between growth and fertility in the tree (see illustration, p. 33).

Pests and disease

Plants die more often as a result of poor care than fro diseases or attack by pests. Correct care is the best preventive measure against diseases and pests. Wher treating sick plants, avoid the thoughtless use of toxi spray in your garden. Very often biological plant protection agents will do the job and they are also kin toward both plants and the environment.

Damage through the wrong kind of care

This can occur in all plants that are not cared for properly.

Waterlogging

Symptoms: Limp, faded shoots and leaves, often yellow discoloration. Damp soil or compost in large containers. Root tips are brown to black, decayed on the inside (check by pinching the root; healthy roots are light-colored inside).
Cause: Too much watering or too often; absent or blocked drainage holes; no drainage; impermeable growth medium.
Prevention: Water carefully, provide an adequate number of drainage holes and a good drainage layer as well as loose, permeable compost or soil (mix in sand or grit).
Remedy: None.

Drying out

Symptoms: drooping, yellow leaves that dry up at the edges and roll up. Flowers fade and drop off prematurely. The roots turn brown.
Cause: Not enough water on hot

or very windy days; a position is too hot and sunny.
Prevention: Water more frequently during hot periods. I substances that store water wi the soil or compost (for examp loamy soil or humus).
Remedy: Stand the rootstock container of tepid water for several hours. If damage is severe, nothing will help.

Nutrient deficiency

Symptoms: Nitrogen deficienc pale leaves; meagre growth. *Phosphorus deficiency*: bluish-violet leaves. *Potassium deficiency*: weak shoots; browr leaf edges that roll up later on. *Magnesium deficiency:* leaves a yellow to brown with clearly marked leaf veins. *Iron deficien* (chlorosis): leaves are yellow, le veins conspicuous.
Causes: The compost or soil contains too much lime (this prevents adequate absorption c nutrients); soil or compost is to compact or hard; not enough fertilizer.

vention: Loosen the soil once
month using a rake; water with
rainwater; proper fertilizing.
Remedy: Provide the missing
minerals. Remove the top layer of
soil and replace it with a new layer
containing mineral fertilizer.

Clematis wilt

Symptoms: Sudden death of
healthy shoots.
Infested plants: Clematis hybrids;
wild species are not so
susceptible.
Prevention: Ensure adequate
moisture during the growth period.
Remedy: None known at present.

Fungal diseases

Black spot

Symptoms: Small, blackish,
round spots on leaves which die
off after a while.
Infested plants: Often roses.
Prevention: Remove damaged
leaves. Spray with mare's tail
brew (see p. 37), repeat at
intervals of several days.
Remedy: Spray, preferably with a
biological preparation, repeat after
two weeks.

Pear rust

Symptoms: Orange-yellow spots
(like rust spots) on leaves.
Infested plants: Pear trees.
Prevention: Ornamental juniper is
an intermediate host for the
fungus, so avoid ornamental
juniper trees in gardens where
pear trees are grown.
Remedy: Spray the pear trees,
preferably with a biological
preparation, repeat in two weeks.

Powdery mildew

Symptoms: a flour-like, white film
on leaves and young parts of
plants. Powdery mildew will also
occur in dry weather.

This pear espalier has been growing here for many years.

Infested plants: Fruit trees, grapevines, roses, cucumbers. Powdery mildew will only be transmitted between plants of the same species.
Prevention: Ensure a well-ventilated position; spray several times with mare's tail brew (see p. 37) at intervals of a few days.
Remedy: Spray with preparations containing dinocap (see p. 37).

Downy mildew
Symptoms: whitish-yellow fungus spots on uppersides of leaves; a white fungus film on undersides of leaves. Occurs mainly in wet summers.
Infested plants: Roses, grapevine.
Prevention: A well-ventilated position. Spray with mare's tail brew at intervals of six weeks.
Remedy: Spray, preferably with a biological preparation (ask at your garden center), repeat again after 10-14 days.

Trumpet vine is a fast-growing climbing plant.

Pests

Aphids
Symptoms: Black or green aphids on shoots and buds. Damage caused through sucking sap visible on leaves, stalks, and branches and can cause them to wilt and die. Rolled-up leaves. Infested plants: Roses, fruit trees, annual climbing plants, honeysuckle.
Prevention: Ensure a balanced nutrient supply as overfertilized plants are particularly susceptible to infestation by aphids. Fermented or fresh nettle brew (see p. 37) will strengthen the plant's resistance.
Control: Spray with tansy brew (see p. 37), repeat every few days; spray with agents containing pyrethrum (see p. 37).

Spider mites
Symptoms: The plants look limp, the leaves dry up and drop off. Small white spots on the leaves, gossamer-fine webs underneath.
Infested plants: Nasturtiums, honeysuckle, clematis hybrids, climbing roses, grapevine.
Prevention: Spray with nettle and mare's tail brew (see p. 37).
Control: Spray with an agent containing pyrethrum.

Codling moth and sawfly larvae (in apples)
Symptoms: To begin with, tiny eggs on the fruit, later holes in the fruit flesh and core; red-brown excrement at the entrances.
Infested plants: Apple trees.
Prevention: Remove all windfalls. Spray with tansy brew.
Control: Employ agents containing pyrethrum.

Scale insects
Symptoms: Light to dark brown scales stuck firmly to leaf undersides and leaf stalks. Damage caused by the sucking of sap from branches and stems.
Infested plants: Fruit trees, roses.
Prevention: Spray with tar-oil winter wash or tansy brew, repeating in several days.
Control: Brush down stems; spray with tar-oil.

Biological plant protection

Plant brews can be sprayed as a preventive and to protect against pests and fungal infections. Fermented plant brews are used as additional fertilizer to mineral and organic fertilizers, to strengthen and fortify plants.

...ssionflower is a spendid flowering climber.

...nt brews

...eparation: 2¼ pounds (1 kg) ...sh, coarsely chopped leaves or ...ounces (200 g) dried leaves in ... gallons (10 liters) cold water. ...ave to soak for 24 hours, then ...il for 30 minutes. Let cool, ...nove scum, and use up quickly. ...ute the brew with water in the ...io of 1:2. This method can be ...ed to prepare the following ...otective and fortifying brews:

...ttle brew has a strengthening ...d fortifying effect and is good ...controlling aphids.

...nsy brew for controlling all ...ids of insects (aphids, insect ...d moth larvae), leaf spot ...sease, and mildew.

...are's tail brew for controlling ...ider mites and mildew.

...rn brew (made from ...*yopteris*), undiluted: use as a ...evention against scale insects.

Fermented herbal brews

Preparation: 2¼ pounds (1 kg) fresh, coarsely chopped leaves or 7 ounces (200 g) dried leaves in 2½ gallons (10 liters) cold water (preferably water that has been left to stand or, better still, rainwater). Leave the brew to stand in the sun (in a wooden or plastic container, never in a metal container). Fermentation will begin after two or three days. Stir thoroughly once daily. A fairly bad smell will be produced. The fermented brew will be ready to use after two or three weeks. Remove the scum, dilute the fermented brew with nine parts water and water the plants. This recipe can be used to prepare the following fermented plant brews:

Fermented nettle brew promotes resistance to disease, contains nitrogen and has a soil-balancing effect.

Fermented borage or comfrey brew contains large amounts of nitrogen and potassium. It is good for vigorously growing plants with lots of flowers.

Biological plant protection agents

Several such preparations can be bought from garden centers. They consist of herbal extracts, algae additives, or pure chemical elements like sulphur or boron. The substances contained in these preparations can be present singly or mixed together. They are used mainly as brews for spraying.

Always follow the manufacturer's directions when using them as some biological plant protection agents, for example pyrethrum, are toxic.

Pyrethrum agents contain pyrethrum which is obtained from a species of chrysanthemum. It is used to control aphids and mildew. It is not dangerous to bees.

Sulphur and dinocap preparations are used to control fungal infections.

Other herbal extracts, usually combined with sulphur or dinocap, can be used for controlling pear rust, mildew and scale insects.

NB: Never spray plant extracts in bright sunshine as they may cause the leaves to burn. Preferably spray under a cloudy sky, in mornings or evenings.

Warning: Children and domestic pets should be kept away when any such products are being sprayed.

Popular climbing plants and espalier fruit trees

The following pages present a selection of profusely flowering, easy-to-care-for climbing plants and varieties of espalier fruit, with photographs, descriptions, and special notes on the correct care of each plant.

ssary of keywords

first name is the common
ne, which is followed by the
anical name (genus and
cies). The introduction gives
ails of the plant's climbing
nnique, its appearance, shape
growth, and any individual
racteristics.
gin: An important clue to the
rect care of the plant.
wer/fruit: The main flowering
e as well as details of flowers
d the formation of fruit.
sition: Information on
uirements in respect of
perature, wind, amount of
light, and the right side of the
se.
l: Advice on soil consistency in
open and for compost in
ntainers.
ter: Tips on proper watering.
tilizing: Information on how
en to fertilize and what to use.
ther care: Special tips on care
d details on climbing aids (if
essary).

arbor with clematis
ors covered in greenery create
ranquil atmosphere.

Diseases/pests: Only given if the plant is particularly susceptible to certain diseases or pests (see also p. 34).
Overwintering: Only for plants that can be grown in a large container (see also p. 29).
Use: Only given if the plant is particularly suited to a certain manner of climbing/covering.
My tip: Extra tried and tested tips on care.

Key to symbols

 Position for the plant: south-facing, sunny.

 Position for the plant: west- and/or east-facing, semi-shady.

Position for the plant: north-facing side, shady.

This plant is also suitable for a large container.

This plant is toxic.

Black-eyed Susan is ideal for balcony boxes.

Cathedral bell is a tireless bloomer.

Black-eyed Susan
Thunbergia alata

This annual winding plant, with heart-shaped, long-stalked, dark green leaves, will grow up to 7 ft (2 m) tall. It is a pretty, delicate summer-flowering plant.
Origin: Southeast Africa, Madagascar.
Flower/fruit: Midsummer to mid-fall, funnel-shaped, yellow to orange single flowers with a dark center, 2 in (5 cm) across. Fruit: Pea-sized, winged capsule with four seeds.
Position: Warm, sunny and sheltered from wind, south-facing.
Soil: Rich in nutrients and humus, standard compost in large container, loose growing medium.
Water: Water regularly but avoid waterlogging.
Fertilizing: In a large container and in open soil, every two weeks with liquid fertilizer; nettle brew also suitable.
Further care: Use twine or a stick as a climbing aid. Tie the shoots to begin with. Pinching out shoot tips once will encourage the plant to branch out. Spacing of plants 24-32 in (60-80 cm).

Cathedral bell, cup and saucer vine
Cobaea scandens

This graceful annual grows up to 13 ft (4 m) tall. Its leaves are feathered and reddish when shooting. The leaf ends have been adapted into tendrils.
Origin: Mexico.
Flower/fruit: Flowers from midsummer to the first frost. Bell-like flower, first whitish-green, later violet. White, red and blue varieties exist. Fruit: 2-2½-in (5-7-cm) long, oval, with three grooves.
Position: Sunny, south- and west-facing walls.
Soil: Rich in nutrients, permeable. Can be grow in compost in a large container.
Water: In open soil or container, water plentifu during the summer.
Fertilizing: In open soil, two to three times durin the summer; every two t three weeks with compound fertilizer in a pot.
Further care: Requires taut wires, twines or sticks as a climbing aid. Pinching out shoot tips encourages branching and formation of flowers Space plants 24-32 in (60-80 cm) apart.
Use: As a visual screen, for covering a wall or in pots on a balcony.

Scarlet runner beans are both decorative and useful.

Nasturtiums will flower all summer long.

Scarlet runner bean
Phasaeolus coccineus

Annual winding plant, up to 13 ft (4 m) tall. The leaves are soft and feathered, with three lobes.
Origin: South America.
Flower/fruit: Red flower, from early summer to mid-fall. Green bean pods, up to 12 in (30 cm) long from midsummer to late fall. Seeds pink to violet, edible.
Position: Sunny to semi-shady; south- and west-facing walls.
Soil: Deep, rich in nutrients. Use fertilized standard compost in a large container.
Water: Water plentifully during the summer; when the weather is very dry, water daily both in large containers and open soil.
Fertilizing: Three times during the growing period, using compound fertilizer. In a large container, every six to eight weeks with compound fertilizer.
Further care: Will require a climbing aid such as wire, a stick, or twine. Space plants 10-12 in (25-30 cm) apart.
Use: Beans for soups, salads, as a vegetable.
Warning: Green beans are toxic if eaten raw.

Nasturtium
Tropaeolum

Plant with tendrils and large, long-stalked leaves (up to 3 in/8 cm across). Hybrids of *T. majus* and *T. peregrinum* are sold.
Origin: South America.
Flower/fruit: *T. majus* has yellow to carmine red flowers from early summer to mid-fall. Fruit: up to ¾ in (2 cm), light green to yellow, ridged. *T. peregrinum* has very feathery, yellow flowers from midsummer.
Position: In full sunlight, on south- and west-facing sides of the house.
Soil: Loose, permeable garden soil, or standard compost in a container.
Water: Water plentifully in a large container; in open soil, daily in summer.
Fertilizing: Potassium- and phosphorus-rich fertilizer encourages flower formation. Begin fertilizing when plants in open soil start flowering; every six to eight weeks in a large container.
Further care: Requires a thin grid or wire fence as a climbing aid. Space plants 40 in (1 m) apart.
Diseases: For aphids, spray plants two or three times with tansy brew.
Use: Excellent for covering composting bins or fences.

41

Ornamental gourds will cover fairly large areas with greenery.

Cucumbers provide fresh ingredients for salads in the summer.

Ornamental gourd
Cucurbita pepo var. *ovifera*

A fast-growing, summer plant with tendrils (up to 27 ft/8 m tall). Leaves 4-8 in (10-20 cm) long; makes a good visual screen. Colorful fruit.
Origin: South America.
Flower/fruit: Mid-summer to mid-fall; large, funnel-shaped, yellow flowers. Popular with bees. Conspicuous fruit which can be kept for a long time as indoor decoration.
Position: Sunny, south- and west-facing walls.

Soil: Nutrient- and humus-rich soil, best mixed with compost. Use standard compost when growing this plant in a large container.
Water: Plentifully to prevent drying out.
Fertilizing: Every four weeks with compound fertilizer during the vegetative phase in open soil; weekly with liquid fertilizer in a container.
Further care: Requires only twine or another simple climbing aid. Space plants about 7 ft (2 m) apart.
Use: Very good for covering a large area with greenery. Grow on a frame over a compost heap to provide shade.

Cucumber
Cucumis sativus

This plant grows quickly (up to 13 ft/4 m), with green tendrils in summer and large, rough, hairy leaves. Many different varieties.
Origin: Western India.
Flower/fruit: early to late summer, golden yellow flowers ¾ in (2 cm) across with pointed petals. Separate male and female flowers. Popular with bees.
Fruit: A green cucumber.
Position: Sunny, sheltered from wind, south-facing wall.
Soil: Humus- and

nutrient-rich; mixed with compost in a container.
Water: Keep evenly moist. Use water that has been left to stand for a day or more. Dryness will make the fruit bitter.
Fertilizing: In open soil, use diluted, fermented nettle brew two to three times during the vegetation phase (see p. 37) or use compound fertilizer. If grown in a large container, use dissolved compound fertilizer every 21 days.
Further care: It will require twine or a frame to hold onto. (Try builder's concrete reinforcing mesh.) Space plants 3 ft (1 m) apart.
Use: For salads.

The flowers of the convolvulus close up at night.

Morning glory needs nutrient-rich, loose soil.

onvolvulus ☠
onvolvulus
epium

iis annual, left-winding
ant with arrow-shaped
aves will grow 3-10 ft
-3 m) tall.
rigin: Central Europe.
ower/fruit: Late spring
early fall, white or pink
iblet-shaped flowers
-2½ in/5-7 cm long).
ie flowers close at night
d in bad weather. Fruit:
ipsule-shaped, pointed,
th four to five seeds.
ision: Sunny, west-
d east-facing walls.
il: Nutrient-rich tending
loamy. In a large

container, mix standard
compost with some loam.
Water: Keep moist; water
well in both open soil and
a large container if the
weather is dry.
Fertilizing: In open soil,
every eight weeks with
compound fertilizer during
the vegetation phase;
every four to six weeks
with compound fertilizer if
grown in a container.
Further care: Requires a
stick, frame, or twine for
climbing. Otherwise fairly
undemanding. Space
plants 24-32 in (60-80 cm)
apart.
Use: Very picturesque as
a covering for a fence.
NB: Contains tannins and
resins.

Morning glory ☠
(*Ipomoea tricolor*)

This mainly winding
species is fast-growing,
up to 17 ft (5 m) tall.
Broad, heart-shaped
leaves, often with three
lobes. Well-known
varieties: *I. tricolor* and *I.
purpurea*.
Origin: South America.
Flower/fruit: Funnel-
shaped single flowers,
4 in (10 cm) across, from
midsummer to early fall,
white with a blue edge. *I.
purpurea* has delicate
violet flowers. Paper-like,
brown fruits, brown
seeds.

Position: Warm, sunny
and sheltered from wind,
south- and west-facing
walls.
Soil: Nutrient-rich, loose
garden soil with compost;
also in large containers.
Water: To protect the soil
from drying out, water
daily during the summer;
twice daily in a container.
Fertilizing: In a large
container, once or twice
weekly; in open soil, once
during the vegetation
phase with compound
fertilizer.
Further care: Sensitive to
wet, cold weather. Spray
with tansy brew or
pyrethrum preparations as
prevention against red
spider mites. Space plants
8-10 in (20-25 cm) apart.

Sweet peas come in many varieties.

The flowers are favorites for vases.

Sweet pea
Lathyrus odoratus ☠

This summer-flowering climber can grow up to 7 ft (2 m) tall. Its paired, feathery leaves end in tendrils. The genus includes about ten climbers and also some low-growing species. It is a very popular plant on account of its delicate fragrance and attractive flowers. Many sweet peas flower best during days with many hours of light, which means that, in the fall, they flower less and less until they finally die.

Open-soil varieties and also some for planting in large containers: Cuthbertson sweet peas, Spencer varieties and Zvolaneks Colossals with particularly large flowers on long stalks.
Origin: Southern Europe.
Flower/fruit: midsummer to mid-fall, colors range from white through yellow and pink to lavender and deep violet. The flower is delicate and usually has spurs and lateral wings. Strongly scented. Fruit: 2-2¾-in (5-7-cm) long pods which turn brown when ripening. They contain spherical seeds.
Position: Warm, sunny and sheltered, cannot cope with draughts.

South-facing wall or fence with sufficient shade from the sun. Cannot cope with direct, intense sunlight at midday.
Soil: Nutrient-rich, permeable garden soil. Chalky soil preferred. In a large container, use loose compost.
Water: Keep evenly moist; sensitive to drying out. Cover the soil with mulch. Never let the planting container dry out.
Fertilizing: High demand on nutrients. In open soil, water with fermented nettle brew once or twice weekly. Always use organic fertilizer. Use liquid fertilizer once or twice weekly in a large container.

Further care: Will require climbing aids like strings, brushwood, sticks, chicken wire, or a delicate frame as the tendrils cannot cope with very thick supports. Always remove all wilted flowers as soon as possible to ensure continuous flowering. Space plants 6 in (15 cm) apart.
Use: For covering a balcony in greenery, in boxes or pots, on a fence, or as a visual screen along the edge of the patio.

My tip: If you cut the flowers early in the morning, they will last longer when arranged in a vase.

Dutchman's pipe will also grow quite happily in the shade.

The flowers of the honeysuckle spread their strong fragrance in the evening.

Dutchman's pipe
Aristolochia macrophylla

This tall winding plant has conspicuous leaves, 12 in (30 cm) across, that are soft and heart-shaped. It is green throughout the summer and grows up to 33 ft (10 m) high. It will provide a good visual screen with leaves that overlap like roof tiles. Other useful species are *A. moupinensis, A. tomentosa.* This plant is quite happy in a town.
Origin: North America.
Flower/fruit: Late spring to midsummer, the inconspicuous, small, yellow-green flowers do not appear until about the third to fifth year. They form insect traps. Fruit: a 4-in (10-cm) long capsule.
Position: Shady to semi-shady, north- or east-facing site.
Soil: Loose, nutrient- and humus-rich. Will also cope with chalky soil.
Water: Requires plenty of water; the soil must never be let dry out.
Fertilizing: Young plants two to three times per year with compost and organic fertilizer; older plants twice with compound fertilizer.
Further care: Requires climbing aids. Space plants at 7-10 ft (2-3 m).

Honeysuckle
Lonicera 💀

This vigorously growing winding plant is usually green during the summer and grows 10-20 ft (3-6 m) tall. There are many species.
Origin: Central Europe, western China.
Position: Sunny to semi-shady, south- and west-facing sites.
Soil: Undemanding.
Water: Avoid drying out during the summer, otherwise there is a risk of infestation with aphids.
Fertilizing: Compound fertilizer once a year in open soil; in pots, every four weeks with compound fertilizer.
Further care: Cut back to prevent bareness from below, requires taut wires or sticks as a climbing aid. Space plants 7-10 ft (2-3 m) apart; individual planting preferred.
Overwintering: In large containers with winter protection (see p. 29).
Warning: Toxic berries!
Species: These include(:)
L. caprifolium: yellow/white flowers
L. heckrottii: reddish flower
L. henryi: red/yellow flowers
L. periclymenum: yellow/white flower
L. tellmaniana: orange flowers

"Lawinia" unfolds large, scented flowers.

"White Cockade" is eminently suitable for displaying in a vase.

Climbing roses
Rosa

Depending on the variety, this makes a 7-17 ft (2-5 m) tall rambling plant. The bush is green during the summer and grows vigorously, with annual shoots up to 17 ft (5 m) long. Its thorns are the actual climbing mechanism of the plant. The leaves are shiny, dark green, and slightly serrated. They remain green for a long time in the fall.

Origin: Crosses from cultivars and from Far-Eastern wild species.

Flower/fruit: Single flowering from late spring to early summer; continuous flowering from early spring to mid-fall; no flowers until the second year, singly or in bunches, single or double; white, yellow, pink or red flowers with many yellow stamens. Some varieties are scented. Popular with bees. Red, berry-like fruit (hip) from late summer to early fall with numerous, small, yellow seeds. The fruit can be used to make jelly, tea, wine and syrup cordials.

Position: Sunny, south- and west-facing sites, sheltered but not too sheltered from wind (not enough circulation of air will create susceptibility to fungal infections).

Soil: Nutrient-rich, loamy humus.

Water: Plenty during the first year and during drought in open soil; water regularly in large containers. Avoid waterlogging. Leave the rootstock to soak in a bucket for several hours before planting and water well again after planting. When watering, water the roots but not the leaves.

Fertilizing: Regularly in open soil, from spring to late summer with rose fertilizer. In a large container, every four to six weeks during the same period.

Further care: Tie shoots to a climbing aid. Cutting out shoots that have finished flowering will encourage continuous flowering roses to produce further flowers. Cut back well in the spring. Space plants 7 ft (2 m) apart.

Diseases/pests: Susceptible to fungal diseases. For prevention and control see page 35

Overwintering: In open soil, heap up soil around the roots and cover shoots with brushwood straw. For large container plants, line the pot with polystyrene sheeting and also cover the shoots with straw and tie this in place

"Golden Showers" flowers continuously.

"Rosenresli" is a robust climbing rose.

Varieties:

Red flowers:

"Flammentanz:" blood red, double flowers, flowers once, up to 13 ft (4 m) tall, spreading growth, robust and hardy.
"Gruss an Heidelberg:" blood red, double, like cultivated rose, large flowers, scented, continuous flowering, vigorous growth, up to 7 ft (2 m) tall.
"Sympathie:" velvety dark red, double, flower like a cultivated rose with strong scent, continuous flowering, up to 10 ft (3 m) tall. Robust variety.

Pink flowers:

"Chaplin's Pink Climber:" dark pink, strongly colored, very large flowers, profusely flowering, semi-double, early flowering. Very vigorous growth, cut off shoots that have finished flowering.
"Coral Dawn:" coral pink, double flowers, like cultivated rose, scented, continuous flowering. Up to 10 ft (3 m) tall. Flowers last quite a long time.
"Dorothy Perkins:" cherry pink flowers, small, but profusely flowering, scented. Up to 7 ft (2 m) tall.
"Lawinia:" pure pink, large double flowers, scented. 7-10 ft (2-3 m) tall. Flowers several times, grows vigorously. Very weather-hardy.
"Rosenresli:" To begin with, salmon red, then salmon pink flowers, large, loosely double. Scent of tea roses. Up to 7 ft (2 m) tall. Not susceptible to disease.

Yellow flowers:

"Casino:" yellow, large, double flowers, scented, continuous flowering. Up to 8 ft (2.5 m) tall, strong.
"Coupe d'Or:" golden yellow, large flowers, profusely flowering, for east- and west-facing walls.
"Golden Showers:" lemon yellow, double flower, scented, continuous flowering, up to 7 ft (2 m) tall.
"Goldstern:" deep golden-yellow, similar to cultivated roses, double flower, continuous flowering. Up to 7 ft (2 m) tall, robust.

White flowers:

"Fräulein Octavia Hesse:" pure white flowers, early flowering, vigorous growth, cut shoots sparingly.
"Ilse Krohn Superior:" pure white, double, like cultivated rose, continuous flowering, strongly scented, profusely flowering. Up to 7 ft (2 m) tall, robust.
"White Cockade:" white, like cultivated rose. Intense scent. Flowers several times, grows vigorously. Good cut flower.

Ivy can live for hundreds of years.

The flower umbels smell faintly of honey.

Ivy
Hedera helix

Ivy is an evergreen climber that can attain heights of up to 10 ft (30 m) with the help of its suckers. It is the only indigenous European plant with root suckers but it can also grow as a ground cover plant in woodland. The leaves of the young plant have three to five lobes, are dark green with white veins and lose the lobes with age. When very old, the shoots of an ivy may be as thick as a human arm. It can live for several hundred years. To begin with, growth is relatively slow. Recommended species include *H. colchica* "Arborescens," with its early flowers, which will attain a height of no more than 60 in (1.5 m); *H. helix* "Goldheart" with small, yellow leaves; *H. hibernica* which has larger leaves than *H. helix*, is more sensitive to frost and rarely produces fruits.
Origin: Central Europe, North Africa, Asia.
Flower/fruit: Early to mid-fall, inconspicuous, green/yellow, semi-spherical flower umbels that smell faintly of honey. Flowers do not appear until the plant is five to ten years old. The berries are popular with birds.
Position: Semi-shade, shade, north- and east-facing walls. Bright south-facing walls are too hot.
Soil: Humus-rich, slightly sandy, loamy soil; loamy standard compost in large containers.
Water: Water well in a large container and in open soil during dry weather and in the fall, otherwise keep fairly moist. Ivy loves high humidity, so enjoys the shade of trees.
Fertilizing: Not demanding; one to two doses of compound fertilizer during the vegetative phase in open soil. Every eight to ten weeks in summer give compound fertilizer if grown in a large container.
Further care: Train young plants upwards with the help of a stick. No need to cut back; will cope with a shaping cut. Space plants 3-7 ft (1-2 m) apart.
Use: Eminently suitable for covering undamaged walls and façades, or unsightly sheds.
Overwintering: Give winter protection if in a large container (see p. 29).

My tip: Ivy is a ground-covering plant which will not climb until it meets a vertical obstacle.

Warning: The berries are very toxic!

e flowering racemes of wisteria.

Spindleberry will thrive in the shade.

isteria
isteria sinensis ☠☠

is is a winding plant
at will grow up to 33 ft
) m) tall, with 3-ft (1-m)
ng annual shoots and
ymmetrical feathered
aves.
rigin: North America,
stern Asia.
ower/fruit: Mid to late
ring, numerous, 6-12-in
5-30-cm) long blue
let racemes at five to
years. Delicately
ented. Occasionally,
lvet-haired, 4-8-in (10-
)-cm) fruit pods in late
ring.
osition: Warm, sunny.

South- and west-facing
sites.
Soil: Nutrient-rich,
permeable and humus-
rich. Hates chalk.
Water: Daily during the
summer.
Fertilizing: In open soil,
once or twice during the
vegetation period with
compound fertilizer.
Further care: Requires a
stable wire as a climbing
aid; cut back after
flowering; shortening
young shoots during the
summer will encourage
the formation of lots of
flowers. Space plants
7-10 ft (2-3 m) apart; it is
better to grow plants
individually.
Warning: All parts of this
plant are toxic!

Spindleberry
Euonymus fortunei ☠☠

This evergreen shrub
climbs with the help of
root suckers and can
grow to about 7 ft (2 m)
tall. Depending on the
species, the foliage is
light green, variegated
yellow or dark green.
The leaves are ¾-2½ in
(2-6 cm) across and
generally red in winter.
Origin: Eastern Asia.
Flower/fruit: Late spring
to early summer,
greenish-yellow flowers
grouped in umbels.
It sometimes produces
white fruit with orange

red toxic seeds.
Position: Semi-shade,
shady, north- and east-
facing sites.
Soil: Humus-rich, loamy,
with a high content of
lime. In a container, in
loamy standard compost.
Water: Water well during
the fall and winter.
Fertilizing: In open soil,
two to three times a year
with organic fertilizer. In a
pot, every six weeks with
a compound fertilizer.
Further care: Will need a
climbing aid. Avoid
cutting back as the plant
gets older. Space plants
5-7 ft (1.5-2 m) apart.
Overwintering: In a pot
with winter protection.
Warning: The seeds are
toxic!

49

The fall coloring of Parthenocissus tricuspidata ranges from yellow through orange to red.

Virginia creeper
Parthenocissus

A climbing shrub which is green in summer. Some can grow more than 33 ft (10 m) tall without any climbing aid. They anchor themselves to any support, using tendrils that have been converted into adhesive pads. Two species are most common: *P. quinquefolia* and *P. tricuspidata*. Both can cope well with a town or city atmosphere and they are particularly suited to covering large areas of walls and façades with greenery.

Parthenocissus quinquefolia

Fast-growing, 27-40 ft (8-12 m) tall, winding plant, green in summer, with suckers, and sometimes with adhesive pads at the ends of shoots. The leaf is about 4¾ in (12 cm) across, dark green; in autumn an intense carmine red. Also available is *P. quinquefolia* "Engelmanii," 33-40 ft (10-12 m) tall, with adhesive pads at the ends of shoots. Dark red coloring in the fall.
Origin: North America.
Flower/fruit: In summer, inconspicuous flower, whitish-green, with panicles. Strong pleasant scent, popular with bees. Fruit: blue pea-sized berries, much sought after by birds.
Position: Sunny to semi-shady. Fall color will be better in a sunny position. South-, west- and east-facing sites.
Soil: Humus-rich. Use standard compost in a large container.
Water: Water well during drought in any site.
Fertilizing: In open soil, once a year; every eight weeks with compound fertilizer in a pot.
Further care: Young plants require taut wires or a climbing frame. Space plants 7 ft (2 m) apart.
Overwintering: Give protection if in a pot.

Parthenocissus tricuspidata

May grow up to 33-50 f (10 -15 m) within one to two years. Self-climbing the ends of shoots have adhesive pads with whi the plant is able to hold by secreting an adhesive (see p. 9). The leaf has three lobes, is 4-8 in (10 20 cm) wide, bronze colored when shooting, then deep green and shin fall coloring from yellow orange to red. The varie *P. tricuspidata* "Veitchii" widely available from garden centers and is distinguishable from *P. tricuspidata* by smaller, more oval leaves with three lobes.

ood for birds: Parthenocissus quinquefolia berries.

The grapevine bears tasty fruit from the first month of fall onward.

tricuspidata "Veitchii gantea" has broad aves. *P. tricuspidata* 'eitchii Aurea" has ellow green leaves with ddish edges; less gorous than other arieties.
rigin: Eastern Asia.
ower/fruit: early to idsummer, yellowish-een flower, faintly cented, popular with ees. In late summer pea-zed, bluish-black berries en on red stalks.
osition: Sunny, semi-hady, south- and west-cing sites.
oil: Nutrient-rich, deep; se standard compost in large container.
ater: During a drought, ater plants well in large

containers and open soil.
Fertilizing: Undemanding; once or twice annually in open soil. About every four to six weeks with compound fertilizer in a large container.
Further care: *P. tricuspidata* "Veitchii" does not require any climbing aid. It may die back a little due to frost damage but will soon produce new shoots from below. Space plants 7-10 ft (2-3 m) apart.
Overwintering: Give protection to containers.
Use: All forms of *P. tricuspidata* are suited to growing in containers. *P. tricuspidata* "Veitchii" will cover even concrete walls with greenery.

Grapevine
Vitis vinifera

This is a vigorously growing plant with suckers, which grows up to 33 ft (10 m) tall. Its annual shoots can be up to 10 ft (3 m) long. The leaves have three to five lobes, are roundish and change color in the fall. For planting in cooler regions, try white or red "Gutedel," "Früher Malinger," and "Früher Blauer Burgunder." Always plant two plants one beside the other.
Origin: Central and southeastern Europe.

Flower/fruit: Later spring to midsummer, small, yellowish-green panicles, slightly scented. Fruit from early fall; grapes with two to four seeds, light yellow or bluish-red.
Position: Sunny, warm, south-facing site; sheltered from wind.
Soil: Nutrient-rich, sandy, loamy.
Water: Undemanding; protect the soil from drying out.
Fertilizing: As a fruiting vine two to four times annually, with mineral fertilizer.
Further care: Cut back to a few shoots in mid-winter. Space plants 6-17 ft (2-5 m) apart.

51

Kiwi fruit requires a warm, sunny position.

Russian vine unfolds delicately scented flowers.

Kiwi fruit, Chinese gooseberry
Actinidia chinensis

This is a fast-growing, left-winding plant, green in summer, 13-27 ft (4-8 m) tall. The leaves are undivided, with serrated edges. Plant both female and male plants to obtain fruit. Suitable for a city climate.
Origin: Southeast Asia.
Flower/fruit: During late spring to early summer, white flowers appear, 1¼ -1½ in (3-4 cm) across, pleasantly scented, turning yellow toward the end of the flowering period. The fruit grows to a maximum of 2 in (5 cm), from late summer.
Position: Warm, south-facing.
Soil: Nutrient- and humus-rich with very little lime in open soil; standard compost in a large container.
Water: Never let the soil dry out.
Fertilizing: In open soil during the summer, every six weeks with compound fertilizer. In a large container, every month.
Further care: Requires a climbing aid. Cutting back annual shoots encourages more flowers. Space plants 3-7 ft (1-2 m) apart.
Overwintering: Provide winter protection in a pot.

Russian vine
Fallopia baldschuanica

This climber can reach up to 27-50 ft (8-15 m). It is a winding plant. The young leaves are reddish, later light green, and turn yellowish in the fall, heart-shaped and 1½-3½ in (4-9 cm) long.
Origin: Eastern Asia.
Flower/fruit: Midsummer to mid-fall, white, 6-8-in (15-20-cm) long panicles with a slight scent. Popular with bees. Flowers from the second year onward. Fruit: from early fall, winged brown nut, eaten by birds.
Position: Sunny to semi shady, south-, west- and east-facing sites.
Soil: Open soil should be humus- and nutrient-rich, standard compost in a large container.
Water: In a large container, daily during the summer; open soil should not be left to dry out.
Fertilizing: In a large container, every second to fourth week until the end of summer. In open soil, twice with annually compound fertilizer.
Further care: Strong climbing aid required. Cut back in spring. Space plants at 7-10 ft (2-3 m).
Overwintering: In a large container provide winter protection (see p. 29).

*nter jasmine will begin to flower from the last month
winter onward.*

The fruit of the hop is also much in demand for flower
arranging.

inter jasmine
sminum nudiflorum

is rambling plant is
een in summer, with
ght green leaves and
ng, arched and trailing
oots. Up to 10 ft (3 m)
, a lovely early-
wering plant.
igin: Eastern Asia.
wer/fruit: Depending
the position, early
nter or early spring;
ar-shaped, yellow
wers, 1 in (2.5 cm)
ng, after five years.
uit: rare, black berries.
sition: Sunny to semi-
ady, warm, sheltered.
uth-facing site; west-

facing with protection
from wind.
Soil: Permeable, humus-
rich.
Water: Water well in fall
before frosts commence,
the shoots lose water
through evaporation even
in winter. Also water well
in summer in dry periods.
Fertilizing: Once or twice
annually with compound
fertilizer.
Further care: Climbing
aids required, such as
wires or a climbing frame,
needs tying. Prune in
spring every two to three
years. Space plants
7-10 ft (2-3 m) apart.
Use: Its hanging shoots
make it an ideal covering
for walls and banks.

Hop
Humulus lupulus

This is a 20-ft (6-m) tall,
winding plant. The leaves
are heart-shaped, up to 6
in (15 cm) across and
have three lobes. There
are both male and
female plants.
H. scandens does not
grow as fast nor is it as
hardy as *H. lupulus*.
Origin: Central Europe.
Flower/fruit: Mid- to late
summer, greenish, female,
strongly scented catkins
and male flowers in
panicles. Fruit: almost
cone-shaped, hanging,
from early fall.

Position: Semi-shady,
west- and east-facing sites.
Soil: In open soil, nutrient-
rich, loamy soil; in a large
container, loamy standard
compost.
Water: Water well in dry
weather. Avoid
waterlogging in a large
container.
Fertilizing: In open soil,
once or twice annually;
regularly every six to
eight weeks in a large
container; with compound
fertilizer.
Further care: use a stick
or wire as a climbing aid.
Cut back in fall.
Space plants 7-8 ft
(2-2.5 m) apart.
Overwintering: Provide
winter protection in a large
container (see p. 29).

Clematis montana "Rubens" will produce an abundance of flowers.

Clematis "Jackmanii" bears enormous star-shaped flowers.

Clematis ☠
Clematis
(wild forms)

Almost exclusively at home in the northern hemisphere. This winding plant has green leaves in summer and climbs up to 33 ft (10 m) high. Less vigorously growing clematis species are suitable for large pots.
Flower/fruit: Late spring to early fall, bell-like or open flowers singly or in panicles. The wild forms have abundant flowers. Fruit: feathery.
Position: Semi-shady. The area around the roots must be covered by plants; west- and east-facing sites; south-facing with protection from sun.
Soil: Humus-rich, permeable, moist. Can cope with lime; use standard compost in a large container.
Water: On hot summer days, water daily but avoid waterlogging.
Fertilizing: In open soil, once or twice annually; in a container, every six weeks with compound fertilizer until late summer.
Further care: Requires a climbing aid. Plant deep; the rootstock should be at least 4 in (10 cm) beneath the soil. *C. montana, C.* "Lasurstern" and *C.* "The President" should be cut back after flowering. All other clematis should be cut back in early spring. Space plants at 7-10 ft (2-3 m).
Overwintering: Provide winter protection in a large container (see p. 29). Protect from frost when plants are young.

Warning: All species are slightly toxic!

Clematis ☠
montana

Grows 20-27 ft (6-8 m) tall; leaves reddish-brown when shooting, later dark green. The wild form is generally not available from garden centers, only cultivated varieties. *C. montana* "Rubens" (pink flowering) or *C. montana* "Superba" (white).
Origin: Central China, Himalayas.
Flower/fruit: Late spring to early summer, white flowers, up to 1½ in (4 c▶ across, when the plant i three to five years old; cultivated varieties flowe abundantly.

Traveller's joy, ☠
old man's beard
Clematis vitalba

This tall-growing wild species grows rapidly to over 70 ft (20 m). The ov leaves are up to 4 in (10 cm) long.

rigin: Central Europe.
ower/fruit: Mid-spring
 mid-fall, white, up to
 in (2 cm) across, with
ght scent of almonds,
oduced three to five
ears after planting. Fruit:
om late spring to late
nter, silvery seedheads.

lematis hybrids

e large-flowered
ltivars are more suited
 growing in large
ntainers. Cultivated
ematis varieties have oval
aves 6 in (15 cm) long,
d climb to 13 ft (4 m).
rigin: Usually from
itish and French raisers.
oil, water, fertilizing
d further care: as for
ld varieties.
seases: Clematis wilt.
rnest Markham:" flower:
dsummer to early fall,
6 in (10-15 cm), brilliant
rk violet.
ackmanii:" robust and
rdy. Flower: midsummer
 mid-fall, 4-6 in (10-15
n), abundantly flowering,
olet purple.
asurstern:" Flower: late
ring to early summer;
jain in early fall, 4-6 in
0-15 cm), violet blue.
Jelly Moser:" Flower:
e spring to early
immer, again early fall,
8 in (15-20 cm), pale
nk striped.
he President:" Flower:
rly to midsummer,
ain mid-fall, up to 6 in
5 cm), dark violet.
ille de Lyon:" Flower:
rly summer to early fall,
6 in (10-15 cm), deep
rmine red.

Clematis "Ville de Lyon" forms a thick tapestry of blossom.

Pear flowers are a delight for bees.

Pears will yield lots of fruit on an espalier.

Pear
Pyrus communis

The pear is a 50-70-ft (15-20-m) tall, pyramid-shaped, deciduous tree. The pear can only be pollinated with pollen from other pear trees, so several trees must be planted in the same vicinity. The leaves are roundish-oval.
Origin: Central Europe.
Flower/fruit: Mid to late spring, white flowers with petals up to 1 in (2.5 cm) across. Numerous reddish-yellow stamens. Fruit ripens from late summer to late fall.

Position: Sheltered, sunny, south- or south-west-facing espalier.
Soil: Deep, nutrient-rich, slightly sandy.
Water: Requires sufficient moisture; water well in dry weather but does not like waterlogging.
Fertilizing: Three times with compound fertilizer (in the spring, summer and fall, see apple, p. 59).
Further care: Do not plant in the vicinity of junipers (risk of pear rust, see p. 35). Space plants 3-7 m (10-23 ft) apart.
Use: Suited to growing as a fan-shaped espalier.
Espalier varieties:
"Alexander Lucas:" Flower medium early; large grass green to yellow green fruit, juicy and sweet. Ripens mid-fall. Storage: until early winter.
"Gute Luise:" Flowering time short; fruit: large, green to reddish-yellow, very tasty and juicy. Ripens: early to mid-fall. Storage: until late fall. Good yield and fruit quality.
"Mme. Verté:" Long-lasting flower, good pollen producer; fruit: small, plump, greenish-brown and pleasantly sweet. Ripens: mid-fall to early winter. Storage: until late winter. Regular yield even in unfavorable positions.
"Napoleon's Butterbirne:" Long-lasting flower, robust; fruit: medium-sized, bottle-shaped, ligh green to light yellow, ver juicy and a little sharp. Ripens: mid to late fall. Storage: until early winte High yield.
"Regentin:" The flower is slightly sensitive to frost; fruit: medium-sized, whitish-green, juicy and tasty, a wonderful winter pear. Ripens: mid to late fall. Storage: early to midwinter.
"Williams Christ:" Small, robust flower; fruit: large yellowish-green, very tasty and tender. Ripens late summer. Storage: one to two weeks. High nutrient requirements; no quite hardy in frost.

Peach trees bloom as early as the first month of spring.

The first fruit is ripe by the middle of summer.

Peach
Prunus persica

This deciduous tree, which grows up to 27 ft (8 m) tall, has dark green, longish, serrated leaves. It grows quickly but does not live for very long. Peach trees are self-pollinating so one specimen is sufficient for producing fruit. Bush forms are usually available in the trade. Grown as a cultivated variety as a peach seedling on light, sandy soils; if the soil is heavy and loamy, a peach scion is grafted on to a plum stock.

Origin: Probably China.
Flower/fruit: From early to mid-spring, ½-2 in (1.5-5 cm) long, dark pink petals. Fruit: midsummer to early fall, varieties with yellow or white fruit flesh. Roundish, yellow to reddish, velvet-skinned fruit with a large, brown kernel. Recently, smooth-skinned varieties (nectarines) are much cultivated.
Position: sunny, warm and sheltered. South-facing site.
Soil: Sandy but nutrient-rich.
Water: Can cope with short-term lack of water but the soil should not be left to dry out.
Fertilizing: Three times during the vegetation period with compound fertilizer, not too late in the fall to guarantee maturing of the wood.
Further care: Cut back in early spring. Space plants 10-17 ft (3-5 m) apart.
Varieties:
"Mamie Ross:" Flower fairly hardy; fruit: medium-sized, light red, striped, slightly sharp taste. Ripens: late spring-early summer. Storage: up to one week. Will still ripen even in cooler areas.
"Mayflower:" Flower, longlasting, early; fruit: small, bright red, striped, greenish-white flesh, velvety skin which pulls off easily. Ripens: mid-summer. Storage: eat fresh. A resistant early variety.
"Proskauer:" Flower small and late, relatively resistant to frost; fruit: medium-sized, flesh yellowish-white, kernel easy to remove, tasty. Ripens: late summer to early fall. Storage: eat fresh. Will still ripen even in regions with a rough climate.
"Weisser Ellerstädter:" flower medium-sized; fruit: large, spherical, yellowish-white with white flesh, kernel easy to remove, tasty. Ripens: early fall. Storage: eat fresh. Resistant to disease; produces abundant fruit.

Apricots, like peaches, bloom early.

The tasty fruit can be frozen.

Apricot
Prunus armeniaca

This deciduous tree grows 10-13 ft (3-4 m) tall, in favorable areas even taller. The wild form was originally a tree of the steppes, so it requires plenty of warmth. The leaves are broad, oval to heart-shaped, dark green with slightly serrated edges. Cultivated trees are grafted onto different kinds of stock, the one most frequently used is the root of a plum tree (advantage: smaller growth). Usually available as a shrubby tree in the trade. Apricots are usually self-pollinating, so only one variety is required to harvest fruit.

Origin: Northern China.

Flower/fruit: Mid-spring, medium risk of frost damage, five white petals up to ¾ in (2 cm) long, numerous yellow stamens. Popular with bees. Fruit from midsummer onward, orange yellow, roundish with a large, brown kernel, fuzzy skin.

Position: Sunny, dry and sheltered. Apart from really warm areas, only recommended as an espalier on the south-facing side of a house.

Soil: Light, sandy but nutrient-rich.

Water: Prefers a dry climate, sensitive to positions that are too moist and which might encourage infestation by fungal diseases (see p. 35).

Fertilizing: Three times during the vegetation period, with compound fertilizer; no later than early fall so that maturing of the wood is not delayed.

Further care: In positions that are at risk from late frosts the flowers can be protected from freezing if they are sprayed with water immediately before the onset of the frost, as the water will then freeze on the flower and the flower will be insulated by its coat of ice. Space plants 10-17 ft (3-5 m) apart.

My tip: The fruit is suitable for freezing.

Cultivated varieties: "Grosse, Wahre Frühaprikose" (early, true apricot): Flower sensitive to frost; fruit: large, oval, tasty. Ripens: midsummer. Storage: eat fresh. Variety with abundant yield.

"Aprikose von Nancy:" Flower medium early; fruit: orange yellow to carmine red, sweet with a fine sharp taste; velvety skin. Ripens: mid- to late summer. Storage: eat fresh. Relatively hardy to frost, high yielding if given a regular pruning.

...ple blossom is enchantingly beautiful with a delicate ...ent.

Espalier apples are often sweeter than those from a tree.

...pple
...alus domestica

...is deciduous tree has ...en an indigenous ...ropean plant for ...ousands of years. It is ...afted onto various ...ocks for a high yield of ...it (see p. 33). It grows ... to 33 ft (10 m) tall but ...n also easily be grown ...an espalier. Numerous ...rieties. Apples require ...llen from another tree, ... try to plant two ...ferent varieties side by ...e.

...igin: Central and ...utheastern Europe.
...wer/fruit: From mid- to late spring, whitish-pink flowers, pink when still closed, up to ¾ in (2 cm) acrsss, with numerous yellow stamens. Popular with bees. Fruit ripens, depending on variety, from midsummer to late fall.
Position: Sunny to semi-shady, east-facing site.
Soil: Nutrient-rich, loose, loamy.
Water: Keep soil moist, protect it from drying out.
Fertilizing: Three times annually with compound fertilizer (spring: for faster growth; summer: growth of fruit; fall: energy loss through harvest). Fertilizing too late in the fall will hinder the maturing of the wood! Also use garden compost as a fertilizer.
Further care: Pruning required (see p. 33). Mulching will prevent washing out of nutrients (use grass cuttings). Space plants 10-17 ft (3-5 m) apart.
Diseases/pests: Guard against mildew by providing a well-ventilated position.
Varieties:
"Berlepsch:" flower slightly sensitive to frost; golden yellow fruit, juicy, tasty. Ripens: mid- to late fall. Storage: until late winter; high yield, resistant.
"Cox's Orange:" late, long-lasting flower; yellow red fruit. Ripens: mid-fall. Storage: until late winter. Wood slightly sensitive to frost.
"Goldparmäne:" flower not very sensitive to frost; red yellow fruit, sweet, tasty. Ripens: mid-fall; Storage: until late winter.: James Grieve": robust flowers; fruit: light yellow to light red, sharp-sweet. Ripens: early to late fall; Storage: six weeks. Rejuvenating cut required! "Klarapfel:" frost-resistant flower; whitish-yellow, slightly sharp fruit. Ripens: mid- to late summer. Storage: three weeks. Disease-resistant variety.

Index

Index

Index

Cover photographs
Front cover: *Clematis.*

Back cover: *Virginia creeper (top), honeysuckle (bottom left), flowering ivy (bottom right).*

Photographic acknowledgements
Apel: p. 7; Burda/mein schöner Garten: p. 17, 21, 37; Busek: p. 2, 14 top, 44 right, 51 right; CD-Photo: p. 49 left; Gruner & Jahr: p. 5; Kögel: p. 24 left, 24 center; Kordes: p. 47 right; Reinhard: p. 3 top, 10, 14 bottom, 40 right, 41, 42 left, 44 left, 46 left, 53 right, 56 left, 59 left
Riedmiller:p. 45 left, 59 right; Sammer: p. 25 center, 42 right, 43 left, 48 right, 50, 53 left, back cover bottom left; Scherz: p. 3 bottom, 16, 25 left, 28, 35, 36, 43 right, 51 left, 52 right, 56 right,   back cover top, bottom right; Schneiders: p. 57 left; Schrempp: p. 58; Seidl: p. 18, 19, 45 right, 48 left, 49 right; Strauss: front cover, 24 right, 25 right, 38, 40 left, 47 left, 54, 55; Wetterwald: p. 46 right, 52 left, 57 right.

This edition published 1996 by Landoll, Inc.
By arrangement with Merehurst Limited
Ferry House, 51-57 Lacy Road, Putney, London SW15 1PR

© 1992 Gräfe und Unzer GmbH, Munich

ISBN 1-56987-695-9

Text copyright ©
Merehurst Limited 1995
Translated by Astrid Mick
Edited by Lesley Young
Design and typesetting by Paul Cooper